MW01051585

I.
Witness

Matthew Edward Clifton

ISBN 978-1-68517-265-7 (paperback)
ISBN 978-1-68517-266-4 (digital)

Copyright © 2022 by Matthew Edward Clifton

All rights reserved. No part of this publication may be reproduced, distributed, or transmitted in any form or by any means, including photocopying, recording, or other electronic or mechanical methods without the prior written permission of the publisher. For permission requests, solicit the publisher via the address below.

Christian Faith Publishing
832 Park Avenue
Meadville, PA 16335
www.christianfaithpublishing.com

Printed in the United States of America

For You, and you.

I hereby swear and affirm all knowledge and information contained herein is true and accurate to the best of my ability, so help me God.
—M. Clifton, witness

I
Witness

Call unto me, and I will answer thee, and shew thee great and mighty things, which thou knowest not. —Jeremiah 33:3

1

Great and Mighty

*Call out to me, and I will answer you, I will tell you great
things, hidden things of which you are unaware.*
—Yirmeyahu 33:3

In the name of Yeshua HaMashiach (Jesus the Messiah) through
the power of the Ruach HaKodesh (the Holy Spirit), I pray to You,
Adonai Elohim, my Lord, my God, faithfully and thankful for Your
wisdom and knowledge. Lord, I wish I could make the entire world
seek after You with a sincere heart, but You say no one seeks You out
without You first seeking out the one.

Although my arrogant heart struggles to accept it, this truth
gives me all kinds of hope when I think about convincing them to
listen. I have faith You will move souls to read and believe in these
ideas, Father, regardless of whether the soul reading this right now
finishes my book or not. Those who are meant to will. I know You
will never force anyone to believe. You don't want a slave. You want
us to choose to love You. It's why You gave us free will.

But will You tell them, God? Will You pique their curiosity by
moving their hearts to wonder if they do decide to listen, You will,
indeed, show them great and mighty things that they do not know?
The things You know I already know. The things You have shown
me.

Help them to believe, Lord, if they call on Your name. Show
them how I prayed this prayer to You (Jeremiah 33:3, quoted at the

beginning of this book and chapter), only a night or two before You showed me what I am going to write about.

You know I'm not stupid, Father. Even though I don't have a formal education. Even though I don't hold degrees in any philosophy, science, or theology. You know the claims I'm going to make will have broad and sweeping impacts on not only those fields of study but on every conceivable worldview known to man.

Still, some will look to dismiss me because of my lack of credentials. Please assure the rest that just because I don't have any degrees, it doesn't necessarily mean I lack knowledge or experience. Please move their hearts to believe wisdom and insight are not exclusive to the college educated.

Others will reject Your truth because of the perceived effects of some trauma on my brain. They'll say I'm broken, defective. Lord, You say through my weakness and imperfection, Your Holy power is demonstrated perfectly. I know I certainly am an imperfect being, though I pray they will find the truth of what I'm saying is beyond rebuke.

Open their minds, Father, if they call on You. God, let me be Your vessel. Let me be the conduit for Your truth. Let me shed my ego and write in Your name, for Your glory, to win souls. In Yeshua's name, I pray. Amen.

2

Truth and Treasure

Everyone lives their lives according to what they believe to be true, but what if what you thought was true was, at best, only partially true? Incomplete? What if there was actually a whole lot more to everything you thought of as real? If I told you I could show you the entire truth, beyond a shadow of a doubt, would you want to know?

Consider these questions carefully, for I believe I have the answer, or part of it anyway, and I will share it with you. There are secrets in this book I think you will definitely want to know about. But first, I need to tell you a little bit about myself.

In 2004, at nineteen years old, bright-eyed, and idealistic, I joined the army as a photojournalist/public affairs specialist. 46Q, pronounced "Forty-six Quebec," was the military occupational specialty (or MOS, army-speak for "job"). The job, or MOS, of a 46Q was twofold. The photojournalist part was just what it sounds like; I took photos and wrote stories covering the scope of army operations.

The second fold, public affairs specialist, was a little more complex. We had our fingers in everything from acting as a liaison for embedded media to creating and maintaining an army presence on newly developed internet platforms called social media (starting with Myspace and Facebook in 2005 and 2006, then all the others as they were developed).

Looking back, I can say my personal life during this time was just as dynamic. On the surface, I always appeared to be a good soldier. Outside of a fight in basic training and a negative review right before I was discharged, I never got in any trouble during my time in the military. Still waters run deep though, and so did some nefarious aspects of my character.

I spent the first four years of my enlistment technically stationed at Fort Bragg, North Carolina, though I was deployed to Iraq for twelve months in 2005 and to Afghanistan for fifteen months in 2007. So with the six months I spent in basic and advanced training and my time in Iraq and Afghanistan, I was really only at Fort Bragg for a little over a year. I have a combat action badge I received from my time in Afghanistan and a set of Airborne wings I earned in between deployments from Airborne School at Fort Benning, Georgia.

I encountered plenty of danger when I was deployed, so to this day, I consider myself extremely fortunate to have not been permanently scarred, physically or mentally, during either of my two combat tours. Quite conversely, I see the difficulties of those deployments as having had an overall positive effect on my character. Make-me-a-man-type adversity. I literally became addicted to working out overseas, so when I came back from Afghanistan (my second deployment), I especially looked the part of the soldier.

Couple my new warrior physique with the help of a friend of a friend, and I landed a job at the Pentagon taking photos for two Secretaries of the Army (Pete Geren and John McHugh). Being The Official Photographer for the Secretary of the Army was a walk in the park compared to my two combat tours. While stationed at the Pentagon, I flew in private jets, stayed at choice hotels, and went to the best restaurants, all while living the easy life, taking pictures of the Secretary of the Army as he traveled the world "touring the army presence."

I've stood in the burial chamber of the Great Pyramid of Giza, placed my hand upon the Sphinx, and walked to the top of the Leaning Tower of Pisa. I have skydived with the Golden Knights (the army's stunt skydiving team) and shook hands with senators on Capitol Hill. I've been in the White House and had a "secret" level clearance. In all reality, my time in the army should have been one of the best experiences of my life. It wasn't.

My clearance wasn't the only secret I held. Concealed beneath the camouflage of my army uniform beat a sinister heart with evil desires. This forced me to assume two lives. One public life, where I was Staff Sgt. Clifton, photographer for the Secretary of the Army, and a second hidden life I lived in the shadows.

By day, I would go to work in the Pentagon, walking by generals and decision-makers. By night, I would be doing things most devious. I wouldn't say I was a double agent. I would say I had split identities. Double lives.

I know, personally, about the two separate lives lived by an addict in denial (a secret life and a public life). Starting at the age of twelve, I made it a habit to use any and every drug I could find. It didn't matter what it was; all that mattered was it messed me up. Man, did I have a split reality going on there for a while!

For every trip I took around the world, touring the army presence, I spent a good month on the couch at my apartment, doing drugs and playing video games. For every positive, gratifying experience I had in the army, there was an even more selfish and humiliating reality that overshadowed and diminished any good thing I had done. I was completely lost in my own drug-addled world, and I hid it well.

Of my eight years of honorable service, I was sober for none of them. Even the initial time I spent in training and my time overseas was polluted with drug use. It didn't matter if there was no apparent way for me to get high or not. I found a way.

In basic training, it was popping caffeine pills secretly purchased at the Post Exchange by a recruit who had the courage to sneak out of the barracks after lights-out and go to the store. When I was overseas, working out and diet pills were on the menu. I had my wisdom teeth pulled in Afghanistan, just so I could get three days off and a prescription for Vicodin.

I had been taking drugs in secret for years, and I wasn't going to let a little thing like being contractually obligated to the army or being deployed to a warzone get in the way of my fun time. I am a very gluttonous person.

In between tours and the entire time I was stationed at the Pentagon, I would routinely drive the five hundred miles home to Northern Kentucky, for three- and four-day passes, the paperwork for which I never submitted for processing, and thus was never charged the leave (or vacation time), I owed for the trips. Sneaky, right?

While at home, I must have spent tens of thousands of dollars on OxyContin (concentrated opiate painkillers I took for fun). About a year and a half before I eventually got out of the army, my secret life exploded into the open when I got into bath salts and spice (manufactured synthetic analogues of cocaine and marijuana you could buy at your local smoke shop).

Bath salts and spice, unlike cocaine and marijuana, do not show up in a drug screen because they are synthetic (made in a lab) analogues (chemically similar to the drugs, but molecularly altered just enough to not be detectable in a drug test). Think of them as fake chemicals that get you high like the drugs they are mimicking, but because they are "fake," you won't "pop hot" on a drug screen, and there are no laws prohibiting their sale.

Both substances were technically legal because as soon as a law was made restricting one analogue form of them, the manufacturers would simply alter the chemicals again, making another analogue different enough molecularly to avoid legal restrictions. It was a clever work-around urinalysis and state and federal drug regulations. I started using these chemicals, thinking it would be safer than using "real" drugs in case the army ever decided to drug-test me. They never did, by the way.

If you don't remember from all the crazy news stories about them in 2011 and 2012, doing bath salts is like doing cocaine, times one thousand. When I did it, I would snort a tiny amount, usually just what would fit on the end of my apartment key. It didn't take much at all, and I would be wired up for the next several hours to days on end. The chemical smell it produced in my nostrils carried with it a distinct burning sensation.

Although it didn't take much to get tweaked out, the drugs caused me to want to take more or "re-dose," which I did routinely. The bath salts also took away my appetite, so I would hardly sleep or eat at all during my binges. At one point, I must have lost thirty pounds. I think the longest I stayed awake was around a week. This was when I was working at the Pentagon!

I would stay up for days at a time, feverishly learning new songs on my guitar or watching immoral videos online, but mostly, I would spend my time playing video games. RPGs (or role-playing games) were my favorite. I was enamored with the immersive fictional world where I could often wield magic powers or super weapons. It appealed to the sense of the supernatural in me, I guess.

These games, if you're not familiar with them, are usually developed for countless hours of gameplay. Doing their own little reward-center-of-the-brain thing, they are designed for players to literally put hundreds of hours of playing time into them. With my supply of "super-coke," free time, and lack of accountability, I did just that.

For the better part of a year and a half (and really if I think about it, it started when I was twelve, smoking weed, drinking, and popping pills), I slowly, but surely, festered a private dependence on drugs that would eventually bleed over into my public life in a devastating way.

About a month or two before it all ended, I started getting very paranoid. It began when I noticed I wasn't receiving any mail in my mailbox, not even junk mail. Suspicious, but nothing to freak out about.

Then I started hearing things, like construction going on in the apartment above mine in the middle of the night, and eventually voices. I will always remember one voice, clearly feminine, said as clear as day, "Does this kid ever sleep?"

I remember cutting the cord of my window-unit air conditioner, thinking the green light emanating from the plug was a camera. Every day, on the days when I did go to work, I was sure it would be the day the army was finally going to spring their trap and nab me. I would literally sweat it out all day (seriously, profuse sweating resulting from the drugs and anxiety of feeling cornered), but nothing ever happened. That was suspicious in and of itself.

I was literally told, "It's okay, you're working," when I apologized for how bad I was sweating on a few occasions. This wasn't out in the field, mind you; this was in the air-conditioned Pentagon. I was only taking photos!

No one ever came after me though, which made me suspect the army. It was either them or they were totally oblivious to my situation. To me, a bunch of field-grade officers and above being so naïve wasn't a possibility.

I thought anyone could plainly see I was going through the tell-tale signs of addiction, but everyone I worked with seemed to have a sense of "I don't care about you, Sgt. Clifton." I mean, they laid it on thick (or at least that was how I perceived it at the time).

One major actually told me it wasn't his responsibility to look after me. He said he had already put in his mentor time. I must have missed the part of the Officer's Creed that says you only care about your subordinate soldiers during certain points in your career.

It was almost like they wanted me to push myself past the point of no return. Like they wanted to just see what would happen when I couldn't take it anymore. One thing they were not going to do is confront me about the issue. Even today, it only makes sense to me in a few ways.

Maybe I was a psychological experiment for them, who knows. Maybe they wanted to see me fail. Maybe they were all too focused on their own careers. Or maybe they just didn't care. It doesn't matter why they neglected me. The important thing to know is the army neglected me.

When things finally came crashing down, it was in the form of a psychotic episode where I thought I was being wiretapped through a light bulb in my apartment. I remember the day I found what I thought was a recording device in one of the light bulbs hanging from my ceiling fan. Sheer drug-induced panic filled me as I made the split-second decision to turn myself in.

I couldn't be sure it wasn't the army watching me, so turning myself in was a calculated risk. If they were responsible, they were probably looking for something else to get me on larger than just drug use; otherwise, they would have made their move by now. Or maybe they were just messing with my mind, seeing how long my brain could be tormented before breaking.

Either way, if it wasn't them, this could be big, so I needed to bring it to someone's attention, fast. No matter what, I knew the army couldn't prosecute me if I voluntarily told them I had a drug problem. It's a catch in their drug abuse policy, which encourages people to come forward and ask for help. So in my head, it was my only option.

I think any rational person would be justified in feeling a little distrustful when you look at the world we live in today. How much more could someone paranoid on stimulants working in the heart of the world's largest and most complex military/industrial engine be? I mean, it is a fact our government has recorded and kept every electronic communication ever sent by anyone in our country. Private citizen or not. Remember Edward Snowden! Privacy, as we used to know it, is now a thing of the past.

The argument, of course, is they archive our communications in the name of our own safety for our own good. I still don't know for sure I wasn't being electronically monitored or psychologically tormented. There are things that still don't add up as far as the light bulb goes.

It was one of those newer style light bulbs, but I still don't understand why there was such a big circuit board inside of it and why there were holes on the top of the plastic base underneath the bulb, unless it was for sound to get through. And why did that one bulb come on just a split second after the three other bulbs in the same ceiling fan? Which is the entire reason I noticed it, to begin with.

I know I must recognize this could all be in my head, so I must dismiss any second thoughts I may still have. I do not know if the army, or someone else, was messing with my head, more so, at least, than I was messing with it myself. I do know now, at least, God was with me then. Even when my mind was gone, He was looking out for my own good. It was a lesson I wouldn't fully learn for yet a few more years.

Anyway, when I turned myself in, it was a Sunday. I went to the post chapel at Fort Myers, Virginia (the army base next to the Pentagon which contains Arlington National Cemetery). I had to go to Fort Myers because the Pentagon didn't have a chapel, per se, and in order to not be prosecuted under the army's substance abuse policy, I had to reveal my addiction to a chaplain or supervisor.

I'm not sure what denomination the chaplain was. He wasn't even supposed to be there at the time. Thank God he was. I remember the look on his face as he took me into his office where I spilled the beans. His reaction was a mixture of empathy and rebuke I didn't quite understand at the time.

We called my father and told him everything, then he made me promise to tell my supervisor at the Pentagon on Monday. Before I left, after calming down substantially, he told me the story of the prodigal son, which I didn't understand at the time either. He asked me what I thought the father said to the wayward son when he came crawling home. I answered he probably told him to get lost.

With a smile, the priest told me no; in fact, the father welcomed the son into his arms with love. I remember thinking at the time, *Yeah right, in what reality did that happen?* I just wasn't ready yet. I wasn't willing to listen.

For a few months, I halfheartedly went to some counseling sessions but remained completely unaccountable to anyone in the army. I still feel like they were complicit in my struggle, if not by actively messing with my mind, then in how they failed to see, or even directly ignored, the telltale red flags of addiction I was waving all over the place. Then again, if you've never been exposed to the reality of drugs, you can't be blamed for not recognizing the signs of a life in downward spiral.

Only days after the light bulb incident, I found myself back in the same old routine of drug use. I had no accountability to anyone, so my lifestyle remained basically unchanged for a few months until I was finally exposed for good and sent to a treatment center about an hour's drive south of the Pentagon in Richmond, Virginia, for a thirty-day inpatient program. Poplar Springs was the name of the facility. You know, now that I think about it, I may have stayed there for sixty or ninety days total.

While at Poplar Springs, I convinced the therapists I needed to be treated for ADHD (attention deficit hyperactivity disorder).

Which meant…stimulants. That's right, folks, I went to a drug treatment facility for stimulant abuse and left with a prescription for stimulants. They were time released; no immediate high like I got from snorting bath salts, but they gave me my fix all the same. Especially when I took a bunch of them at once.

When I returned from the treatment facility, I did an outpatient program for a few weeks at Fort Belvoir, Virginia, I think, before returning to finish the few remaining months of my enlistment at the Pentagon. I remember telling the colonel in the Public Affairs Office that the walk into the Pentagon on my first day back felt longer than the thirty (or sixty or however many) days I had just spent in treatment, and I had to learn this lesson the hard way, but sometimes, that's how we learn the best. All with my prescription in hand.

I was an expert in crafted humility. I still believed I was in control of things. Naturally, I felt humiliated showing my face around the place at all after I had been exposed as a failure, and when I finally left the army for good a few months later, I slinked away without any ceremony or send-off. I was honorably discharged. I left the army with my head down.

To say I was jaded by the time I got out of the army would be an understatement. I told myself and anyone else who would listen how hypocritical the army, not to mention our country, was. I allowed the media to fuel my boiling resentment and disgust with its blatant lies, subtle deceit, and subliminal propaganda.

I questioned my friends during the 2012 presidential season, asking them what was the point of participating in a broken system. I could routinely be heard saying, "I'll vote when I can vote 'no confidence.'" My heart was getting harder. I thought I had kicked the bad drug habit when I came out of treatment before I got out of the army, but little did I know a full-blown heroin addiction was right down the road.

In hindsight, I see I was nowhere near fully healed, not when I got out of treatment and definitely not when I got out of the army. It was easier to blame the whole system that let me fail than it was to look honestly at myself. It wasn't until years later when I came to an understanding about the truth of God, I was able to finally come to terms with who I am as a broken individual.

I was corrupted. I had to learn to let go and give control of my life to God completely and unquestionably. My entire life, I had believed I was special, I was enough. Well, I was half-right at least. I was special, but I was nowhere near enough.

The Bible says where a person's treasure is, there you will also find their heart. This is a bittersweet truth, for while hearts can be found in nearly all manner of depravity, valuing sin and debauchery as treasure, any single person can make the choice to change what they define as valuable and choose to seek true treasure in their life, thus putting their heart in the right place.

The heart may want what it wants, but you have the power to change it! Saint Augustine noted a heart will remain restless until it rests in God. There are so many questions in this life. Too many to answer in a single lifespan. There are also too many paths to follow in seeking the truth. How do we know which route to take to find the ultimate truth, to find God?

Whether we realize it or not, we all spend our time on earth building a metaphorical structure. It is the house of our heart, and it contains our treasure, what we value. It is built on the morals and ethics and with the beliefs each of us lives by. Our own personal code, if you will.

The problem is, however, too many people spend their lives building hearts using shoddy materials, according to their own plans, and in pursuit of their own treasure. They never look to get advice from The Master Heartbuilder and Treasure Hunter. Or if they do seek guidance, they come to realize too late their supposed "master" is actually a fraud.

Though we all build our hearts in seeking our treasure according to our own individual moral code, if we rely solely on our own means and methods (materials and designs) without consideration for God's ultimate master plan (building with the correct materials using a proven design capable of containing true treasure), then we will inevitably find our hearts will not pass inspection when we are finished building. What we thought was our treasures will be poured out on the ground when we die, and we must account for what we built and valued in this world.

It's easy to see the error in building a heart founded on and using the pursuit of drugs or sex or some other obvious sin as your treasure. Bath salts? Video games? Anyone can see how shallow those endeavors ultimately are, but how do you know which worldview, what beliefs in life are suitable materials for building? Which treasures are truly valuable?

Things like family or legacy might seem like solid treasures to pursue in building. They too ultimately prove themselves to be unstable, incomplete. You must seek God. You must build your heart according to Godly pursuits if you wish to obtain and keep true treasure in this life and the next!

Like everyone else, the house of my heart would remain dilapidated until I came to God with my request to renovate. Also, like everyone else, I would remain broken until I turned over control. When I did eventually give up, I was able to give my life to God completely and have never looked back. And that, my friends, was the first step toward the remarkable change and healing I have experienced in my heart as a result of accepting and surrendering myself to Christ.

What kind of heart are you building? Know it's never too late to renovate! All you have to do is turn over control to God, The Master Heartbuilder. It's the easiest and hardest thing you will ever do, but do not fear. He knows exactly what He is doing and will guide your hand and watch over your construction with expert care and attention.

There's no need to be anxious about the "in progress" condition of your heart either. Everyone's heart under His care is in repair. You can be confident in the assurance once construction begins, improvements and upgrades will continue to be added for the rest of your life. Because God loves you, He will not allow a good work begun in you to fail. You can build a house on that promise. Believe it!

3

The Free Gift of Love

Do you know you are loved? It's true. You are unique and special and valued. Yeah, I am talking about God, but also, I am talking about people. At the very least, a person. Someone out there, and I am willing to bet there is more than just one, loves you.

Did someone give you this book? I hope so. This is certainly my intent as an author, that all who read my book receive it as a free gift, and after having read it, if they feel so moved, they would buy at least two copies for others in their lives. Two or more people they love. So you see, someone must love you to have given you this book.

That is the people part. But even if you weren't given this book: let's just say for the sake of argument you found it somewhere (hopefully not the trash can!), the other part, the God part, is better. It's like the people part, but awesome. Divine.

The God part says you receiving this book is not an accident by any stretch of the imagination, but has, in fact, been planned out and mapped into history since before you were born. You might even call it fate. "How can it be?" you may ask. The answers are within, but receiving them will take a little effort on your part.

Whether you know who sent you this book or not, I promise the person responsible for you holding it in your hands at this moment loves you unimaginably. This book is a free gift to you, and if, after having read it for yourself, you feel moved to do so, I would ask that you return the favor. Please consider purchasing a copy or two to give away as gifts to others in your life whom you love. Let this book be a token and representation of your love to others who may benefit from the information and affirmation provided in these pages as well.

If you start reading and realize it's not for you, do me a favor and give the book away. To anybody. God will work His purposes in this life. I encourage you, though, to take the time to examine the words herein. If you just give it a little faith, I think you will find God will bring you the rest of the way.

It's like starting a car to go somewhere. If you don't believe the car will start, you would never try to turn the key, but what if your disbelief in the car's ability to start was unfounded? What if your disbelief didn't have anything to do with the car? What if your disbelief was inside of you?

Would you not believe simply because someone else told you the car wouldn't start or because you noticed it has never started by itself? Why would you believe them without at least trying to turn the key? Why would you assume the car would start on its own without someone there to start it?

God is similar. He won't ignite your life without you first turning the ignition in faith. He won't take you to your destiny, your destination, without you getting in the driver's seat and yielding to His controls and power. Without you taking at least some initiative, I'm afraid the usefulness of the car will be left unrealized in the driveway while you try to walk out your own path in life.

Let this serve as a warning, however, to all who would continue pursuing the secrets of this book. Your reality will be torn to pieces, ripped to shreds. I am sorry, but it can't be avoided, I'm afraid. I am going to ask you to consider some very difficult ideas before this is all over with. I promise to do my best to explain it clearly and in a way that is understandable, but the nature of some of the topics presented is just plain counterintuitive or confusing.

It will not be easy. You cannot build a house without first tearing down the existing structure and clearing out the space to be used. The site must be excavated. Take heart, for what is reality but perception, and what is truth if it doesn't destroy ignorance? Keep reading to find out.

4

Agenda: Search Yourself!

In writing this book I want to explain—everything. I want to present a worldview solid in its logic, comprehensive in its evidence, and conclusive in its result. I want to give you, the reader, a concrete argument that irrefutably explains the truth of experiential reality (the reality we experience), in a manner that would hold up in a court of law. The courtroom in which this book will be judged, however, will not be a court of law. Rather it will be judged in the secret courtroom of your own heart.

My audience is twofold. On one hand, I want to provide a clear and detailed foundation for people of faith to be able to present and defend our belief in God. On the other hand, I want this book to serve as a means of persuasion for those who don't necessarily believe in God but are open to the possibility.

In both instances, I intend to achieve my goal by communicating effectively to both audiences the true nature of reality. This is the truth that has been revealed to me, the main point of this book. The Tri-real Existence is what I call it.

In a nutshell, reality, God, man, and everything else is threefold, or triune. I hope you will find my proofs beyond reproach. This book will give the reader a comprehensive, true description of the reality in which we live.

In understanding the true nature of reality, I will give people of faith a solid foundation for their beliefs while at the same time presenting a verifiable and demonstrable argument for my position, which I hope will win over open-minded skeptics. I intend to ultimately prove the truth of my claims through you, the reader's individual application of the concepts I present.

If you apply what you've learned in this book and are fruitful, hopefully, you will buy at least a few copies for those close to you. This is how I intend to make the information in this book free to all but still hope to support my growing family at the same time. Any and all support is greatly appreciated.

At the conception of this book, I was convinced, and still am, I had been shown a fundamental truth about the nature of reality. I knew I had been given a calling by God to spread this information to the willing world, and there was a part of me that wanted to believe there was some magic word, or combination of words, out there, I could write, which would turn everyone's heart toward my cause, no matter who read this book. I knew my arguments and reasoning were true. I believed this would be enough to unite humanity under an ultimate objective truth finally revealed. I thought I could make people believe.

It didn't take long, however, for the bubble to burst and for me to realize another truth about reality: people will believe what they want to believe, and more importantly, disbelieve what they want to disbelieve, regardless of the truth of the matter or how convincing I may be able to write.

I want to be careful in how I approach some of the topics in this book, so as not to turn off people who might have some ingrained biases toward God or Christ. At the same time, I don't want to spend too much time trying to convince people who aren't going to listen to begin with.

So how do I proceed? The answer came to me from an internet comment. Here is the story:

As I was scrolling through an app I no longer have on my phone the other day, I came across a meme which read:

> *What weight and worth is there in every passage*
> *of the blessed Gospel! Enough, one would think, to*
> *enter and pierce the dullest soul, and wholly possess*

*its thoughts and affections; and yet how often does it
fall as water upon a stone!* (Richard Baxter)

How apt this quote would appear in my feed at the time it did? It made me think of my recent realization about the nature of people's disbelief. I wrote a comment:

*How do you convince someone to listen? Evil is not
our curse; it is disbelief.*

To which the poster of the meme responded:

*God alone softens hearts and opens eyes and ears. We
are just called to share the Gospel. If we faithfully
present the Word of God, we have done our duty.*

So it's out of my hands. All I can do is present the information I have, clearly and concisely, hopefully at least mildly entertaining, and relatable, spiced with personal testimony. There is no need to try to convince anyone of anything. That is up to you and God. I'm just here to tell the story.

I had been clean from heroin for about six months when I first met my wife in 2016. My relationship with God at the time was still in its infancy as well. I believed knowing or believing that God existed was enough to save me. I knew God must exist, but I still had a long way to go to be saved. At the time, I was nowhere near accepting Christ into my heart.

About a year after I met my wife, we moved into a little apartment together in Covington, Kentucky. The guy who lived in the apartment above us, I found out one day, sold more than just weed. He sold everything, including heroin.

That's all it took. I relapsed the first time and got high, no problem. Tried it a second time, and it felt just as good as the first. When I went back the third time, however, it got me.

They say it only takes one time to kill you. I guess I was searching for the one. I almost found it. I overdosed from heroin in 2017, and even though I technically survived, I thought my mind would be damaged beyond repair for the rest of my life due to the time I spent unconscious before my wife (girlfriend at the time) found me and called the paramedics.

I was comatose on the floor of my apartment for at least an hour before my wife came home and discovered me passed out, lying awkwardly on (my God, I can't even remember which arm it was). She called 911 and flushed the drugs I had left, half-used, on the top of the dresser. My wife does not tolerate stupid behavior, but she does love me, and I love her. So much!

My wife saved my life that night. I don't know if I ever even thanked her, but I do know I don't deserve her. She is a gift, a special person indeed. She never let the dinginess or darkness of the bad parts of me outweigh who she saw as a sincere soul desperately seeking God. I will love her forever because of this, but I digress.

The way I had fallen on my arm while unconscious cut off the circulation and caused my hand to become and stay swollen, at least partially, for months after the incident. The feeling in my hand didn't completely return for about a year. The damage to my brain, on the other hand, I figured would last much longer.

It's one thing to appear to be stoic on the outside, but I didn't feel anything, couldn't think *anything* on the inside! I had no inner monologue. I lost my conscience, it seemed, and I would have been scared to death if I wasn't helplessly and hopelessly entertaining the idea my soul may already have died!

When my brother, his name was David, really did die from a heroin overdose only a month or two later, I couldn't even think of anything to say to him in my head as I sat over his lifeless body, my hand gently resting on his icy shoulder, while the coroner prepared to take his corpse away. I wish I had been there for my little brother, but I wasn't.

I found out he died in a text from my mom. I was working for the post office at the time and went to see his body after work on the day he died. With the exception of my relapse and overdose a few months earlier, I was working on leaving heroin behind me. My brother never really wanted to quit.

David had just been released from jail for an incident where he passed out on heroin and wrecked my sister's car. He hurt another person when he did this, so they took him to jail for about nine months as a result. His sentence was just long enough for his tolerance to be lowered to a level where his relapse would be fatal. I can relate. When he died, I thought I was already dead mentally.

For the longest time, I felt so guilty about my inability to grieve for David. My apathy wasn't reserved solely for the loss of my little brother either. As I said, I felt like my spirit had died (a delusion that plagued me constantly for some time after I was delivered from the drugs even, but more about that later). Relationally, I was screwed. I couldn't hold a regular conversation with the people I loved, much less with someone I didn't know.

At David's funeral, I remember feeling more awkward, having to small talk with friends and family, than sad over my brother's untimely demise. I was an anxious wreck that day, not because of the loss of my younger brother, but over the stress of trying to figure out what to say to anyone in response to anything! I remember the few times I was able to muster up some tears. They felt wholly forced and contrived. I knew I was supposed to feel grief, but I just couldn't. It made me feel hopeless. Resigned.

All my relationships seemed like they were going to crumble to dust, much like my broken mind had. My wife's sister told her recently she was worried they lost me then. I thank God every day my wife made the choice to stick it out with me, but it was God who healed me. He showed me the value of the mind and the power of love.

He was with me through all my trials. He walked with me through every one of my tribulations. He brought me back out on the other side, not only as good as, but better than I was before. God restored my mind, and in under two years, I went from being a zombie to writing a book! You need look no further than my own life to see evidence of the miraculous love of God. I will show you.

In the years since God healed my mind, I have, indeed, felt grief for my brother, and it is a joyful grief, at that. Like everything else in my life, God has given me a perspective that results in contentment.

Even during the times I want to worry for David's soul (he was far from a saint and objectively closer to a scoundrel during his time on earth), I find comfort in knowing God's justice is perfect.

Everything in my life and yours too, if you would only believe, has been working toward a greater purpose. I see this in hindsight throughout my life, when I recognize through all my failures and downfalls, I have been led here, now, in relationship with a God who loves me deeply. How can anyone not see it?

The Bible says the evidence for God is written in the stars, meaning if you look objectively at creation, the logic a Creator made it, should be self-evident. As you read through this book, I would humbly ask you to search your own heart and open your own mind to uncover any prejudices or beliefs you have that may stand in the way of you understanding what I'm trying to express.

The mind is invaluable for discerning (figuring out) what is true. I want you to use your mind when discerning the veracity or truth of my claims. I understand I have the burden of proof. I want you to hold the evidence in this book to a high standard, hopefully beyond a reasonable doubt. In the end, I believe I have enough concrete facts, as well as circumstantial evidence, to prove my case.

All the facts and evidence in the world will not be enough, however, if you are not willing to consider the possibilities being presented might be true. If you can do this, then you need only to follow my evidence and logic. Then judge for yourself, using strict but realistic standards.

Again, ultimately, it is up to you. Not even God will force you to believe. I am all for healthy disbelief, but it must be healthy. Otherwise, you are in for a rude awakening when reality finally does decide to crash the party.

It reminds me of a spot I heard on the radio a while ago. It was an excerpt from the Ravi Zacharias program called *Just Thinking*. Part of the Just Thinking ministry is a syndicated fifteen-minute radio program that talks intelligently about Christ and God from philosophical, theological, and scientific perspectives. It is a great and thoughtful ministry.

In this particular segment, an apologetic speaker associated with the Just Thinking ministry talked about the difference between healthy disbelief and unhealthy disbelief. The difference, according to the speaker, is the same as the difference between the skeptic and the cynic.

The Greek word for "skeptic," *skeptomai*, means to search, think about, or look for. The word "cynic," on the other hand, is derived from the Ancient Greek *kynikos*, meaning doglike. It is unclear why this name is used for cynics, though I would suggest it has to do with belief. Dogs will not believe anything they cannot see. Even if it is in front of their faces the entire time. Keep that in mind.

Anyways, as the speaker explains, a skeptic will not believe until presented with enough evidence, while a cynic will not believe no matter how much evidence is presented. He ends the radio program with a question I will repeat. Which one are you: a skeptic or a cynic?

This one aspect of thinking is crucial to what I hope to accomplish with this book. I need you! I need you to read what I have to say and consider what I write with an open mind. I need you to be skeptical, but not cynical. Can you do it? Will you honestly search yourself as much as you search the evidence I present?

5

Prophet Disclaimer

It is at this point I feel I need to take a minute to present what I might as well refer to as the "prophet disclaimer." I want to make a very clear distinction between saying I believe God has shown me a truth and claiming to know what God thinks or will or won't do. I do not claim to have the word of God.

I in no way claim to be a prophet or to have any advance or special knowledge about God's plan or the Bible. I do believe I was shown, by God, the information I hope to share with you in this book in order to spread His truth to those who are willing to listen. Quite honestly, though, half of the time, I tend to operate under the assumption God will have this book fail and maybe there is some lesson I am supposed to learn in the defeat.

Who knows, but I do not want to presume to speak for God. Maybe later, I will tell the story of how this information came to me. I think there were some divine qualities surrounding the event, but never have I ever heard God speak to me verbally, nor have I ever had any vision. Though some of my dreams, but I'm getting ahead of myself.

There may very well be modern-day prophets out there, but I would caution the person reading this. Anyone can say God spoke to them. There are entire religions in this world based on the "revelations" of God given to only one person.

I don't know about you, but I will not risk my immortal soul following the teachings of only one person without some type of collaboration or verification from another primary source. If I were you, I would bounce everything so-called modern-day prophets say off the foundation of truth which is the Bible (66 books, written by around 40 authors, over a period of about 1,500 years, with no contradictions!).

I can hear the gasps now. No contradictions in the Bible? Is he stupid or just brainwashed? To those who say that I say this: I will not answer a fool according his folly, but I will answer a fool according to his folly; let the reader understand the allusion. The Bible is not contradictory. It is, in fact, verified through multiple witnesses.

Forty authors, 1,500 years…not just one guy in a single lifetime! What I am saying, to the best of my knowledge, does not contradict anything in true biblical Christian theology. My special revelation is descriptive only, not prophetic.

I "know" God must exist, but I do not *know* He exists. He has never shown Himself to me, though He shows Himself to me in new glorious ways every single day. I believe with all my heart Yeshua is real, but sometimes, I don't believe it at all!

6

Disbelief

God, help me. It happened again. I woke up this morning, nearly scared to death and panic-stricken, with that sick feeling in my stomach, like everything You've shown me was a lie. Am I lost? I hate this feeling.

Yeshua, it feels like waking up from a bad dream, but in reverse: like waking up *to* the intense fear and confusion of a nightmare! God, why does this happen? Why does my entire reality feel like its unraveling before my eyes when, for those first few brief horrifying seconds, I actually believe in the deepest parts of my being that everything I have come to know as true in this life is actually false?

Lord, where does this feeling come from? Is it the devil messing with me or just me messing with myself? Part of me thinks either my own self-defeating malice or something else's may be using my disbelief to try to stop me from writing.

Fear, doubt, and confusion are trademark signs of the adversary, and making me feel insecure about what I'm writing about would be the only way to stop me, Lord, because intellectually, I know there is nothing out there which can disprove what You have shown me.

Fear. Doubt. Confusion. Yeah, it must be evil. That's why it waits for just the right opportunity to strike, usually choosing a vulnerable moment like it did this morning, immediately after sleep, before my groggy mind has any chance to grab ahold of the concrete beliefs that stabilize my world and anchor my sanity.

I know it's just a feeling. I should know it will soon pass. I know I should know better, of course, but when this happens, it's like what I know doesn't seem to matter. It's like my thinking brain gets shut off or overruled by some evil emotion. A sinister little feeling that bubbles up from the depths of my corrupted heart to keep me from believing what I know in my head must be true.

I hate losing my rationale like this. Why can't I seem to remember the emptiness behind this feeling? Why can't I remember there's never any articulate thought or coherent argument to justify any of it? Just an echoing question/statement stuck in my mind, a double thought, like a broken record that keeps repeating, *What if it isn't true? / It isn't true!*

Of course, I know what You've shown me is true. You are eternally reliable and ever faithful, unlike me. You are certain and unchanging, the guiding light of the world in times of darkness. You are the Truth, and You do not lie.

Daily, Lord, You expose Your truth to me in new and glorious ways. Every day, Yeshua, You show me how perfectly it all fits together. Every. Single. Day. My God, You reveal to me the answers to some of the most fundamental questions of life. You are an amazing God, and You are always with me. Even when I don't feel it.

Father, You promise to give wisdom to those who ask for it, and although I don't want to be presumptuous in assuming I could even comprehend Your reasons for allowing certain things to happen, I would ask You allow me to glean what You will from these encounters with disbelief. Show me on the rare occasions when I do find disbelief in my heart, if I just give it a minute and focus on You, talk to You, the universe will slowly begin to make sense again.

You will soothe my anxiety and comfort me as the world starts to turn once more. My brain will take back control from my hardened little heart as I meditate on Your wonderful mysteries and think through my arguments, searching for critical holes and faults, any blatant omissions, but finding none worth getting worked up over. It is true, after all. I knew that…*I know this*. Yeshua, please help me to believe it wholeheartedly.

Father, please help me remember these things when I occasionally wake up feeling like I'm missing something obvious when I know I'm not. Remind me there is no truth to substantiate that unreal feeling when my deceitful intuition tries to tell me I'm overlooking some vital fact that isn't really there. Lord, please help me remember this feeling is just a feeling and nothing else.

You say to glory in my tribulations, Yeshua, for trials produce patience, and it's in the patient endurance of the valleys of my life, in persevering through my disbelief, I will gain valuable experience based on a hope in You, Adonai, my God. Neither will You make me ashamed of my hope, but rather, You will justify my belief through the abundant shedding of Your love in my heart.

Father, this helps me to take the long view and not worry so much about my disbelief. Your purposes are not always crystal clear to me, Yeshua, but I know they are there for me to figure out. I recognize it's likely You're trying to help me grow by teaching me to overcome my disbelief through turning to You. I'm also confident there are multiple lessons I'm supposed to learn from all this, Lord.

The comprehensive precision of Your truth is amazing to behold. The way it permeates everything it touches perfectly without contradiction, across individual lives and throughout generations and cultures, is a miracle in and of itself, fully worthy of my worship. You are a remarkable God!

When I ponder Your transcendent truths, I must also acknowledge it's entirely likely Your purposes behind my struggle with disbelief don't have as much to do with me as I might like to think, but in fact have as much or more to do with other people, in some enigmatic way, some distant day.

I promise, Yeshua, with Your grace, to continue working diligently toward telling the world what You have shown me. For I know I have work to do. I know what You've shown me is not just for me. I know You want me to share this revelation with the world.

My God, I can foresee all the souls who may come to You as a result of what I could write in my book. Sincere souls desperately seeking answers to questions in their lives. Lord, this insight You have given me answers, or can answer, many of the fundamental questions regarding life and reality, which souls have struggled with for thousands of years. God! There's nothing my disbelief can say to dispute that.

Talking about it helps. Thank You. Although I would like very much for my disbelief to be vanquished instantly, I will remain patient in the assurance You will transform my heart in Your time, not my own. I'm thankful for this. I'm also thankful these mornings of disbelief don't happen more frequently than they do, and they seem to be occurring less often as time goes by.

You know I do not want to disbelieve, Father, so until the day my heart is perfected, I will continue to consciously reaffirm my submission and allegiance to You, Adonai Elohim Tzavot, my God, and to call on the promise of Your Word to dwell within me and enlighten my soul.

So thank You, Yeshua, for reminding me of these facts when I wake up unbelieving like this. Thank You, Lord, for Your Spirit, which gives me the unbounded peace and comfort to persevere through these brief moments of disbelief. Thank You, God, for putting my soul at ease and renewing my mind daily.

Father, please help me to remain single-minded in You. Please continue to soften my heart according to Your will. Lord, help me to stay focused and vigilant regarding the task at hand. Thank You, Yeshua, for this opportunity. Let me bring them to You. Let me give them the answers I know You want me to share with them, and I will.

I am thankful, God, for everything You have done and are doing in my life. I know and will remain confident in Your truth while You work on softening my own heart. I believe this is what You want from me, God, so please help the part of me that wants to disbelieve. With Your blessing and grace, I will spread Your reality to those who are willing to listen. In Your name and for Your greater good and glory. In Yeshua's name, I pray. Amen.

7

Belief

I wonder, are there times when you have wrestled with the same feeling of disbelief? I think most of us go a round or two with this demon at least occasionally in our lives. I mean, surely, we all must have had at least one experience where we couldn't grasp our reality or part of it. Whether it be life-changing news we couldn't believe or a loss we couldn't accept, some struggle more, some struggle less, but I genuinely believe most people must question their reality to some extent, at least some of the time.

What about atheists though? Are they just like the rest of us in this regard? Do they ever feel this way? Do they ever question their beliefs? Or more importantly, do they question their disbelief? One would think, naturally, yes, given the disbelieving nature of their worldview.

Though I must say, I believe their disbelief in God is misplaced. I wonder, like me, do they sometimes wake up in the morning, clearly affected by, but unable to remember, the dream they were just having? Are they roused from their slumber every now and then by an eerie, cold feeling telling them their entire worldview is wrong?

Maybe it's not they don't believe, per se, but they have just succumbed to the emotion of disbelief I struggle with. Could it be agnostics are the ones who are really the slaves to their emotions? At least more so than the religious types they decry?

Maybe because they deny or refuse to search for God, agnostics become captive to their emotions. Maybe there is some perceived enmity or resentment between atheists and God on the atheist's part. Or maybe there really is some enmity there on God's part. The Bible says God allows the eyes of the stubborn-hearted to be closed of their own doing. Maybe there's something to that.

Many nonbelievers say they don't believe in God because of scientific evidence, but I wonder if maybe there is more to their unbelief than scientific evidence. They must put their faith in certain facts that seem to support their position, but what do they think of the multitude of facts which point to God to begin with? Maybe they just ignore them.

I wonder, do scientists ever consider using science to try to prove or disprove the existence of God would be like trying to measure the ocean using a stopwatch? Do they not understand a stopwatch is the wrong tool for the job? Do they really think they can fathom the depths of the sea?

I know God is real in my head more than in my heart most of the time, but apparently, agnostics can't even fathom the intellectual probability of God to begin with! Is that really it though? Do atheists really have scientific evidence that proves there is no God? Or maybe, is it possible in the heart of every die-hard unbelieving soul is a deep-seated resentment being harbored which paints all of their scientific evidence with bias?

You see, the nonbelieving worldview is inherently flawed. Atheists cannot answer fundamental questions about the origins of the universe and life itself. Neither can agnostics adequately explain the existence of meaning or morality. Further, given the unbeliever's dogmatic defense of science as a justifying factor in their worldview, I think their philosophy actually lacks any credible scientific arguments to support any kind of disbelief in a Creator Entity.

Case in point: the big bang theory. This is the end-all-be-all for creation according to atheists, but will it hold up under some scrutiny? Let's see. While this theory most surely can account for the vast expanse of the universe, unfortunately, it cannot explain the creation of the universe itself.

According to nonbelieving scientists, the universe was created from a single point of energy called a singularity, which exploded one day, for unknown reasons, and created the entire universe. Really? A singularity? What a cop-out! Is that the best you can do, atheists? Way to kick the can down the road! What created the singularity, huh?

The first law of thermodynamics states energy in a system can neither be created nor destroyed, only transferred. I will speak more on this later on in the book, but for now, just know the big bang theory cannot account for the creation of the vast amount of energy in our universe.

Similarly, atheists and agnostics masquerading as "objective scientists" will use evolution to try to explain both the origin and vast expanse of life on earth. It does neither actually. An alligator a hundred million years ago is the same as an alligator today, and there are no instances in the fossil record of a beast becoming an alligator, an alligator turning into another kind of creature, or any organism turning from one kind of animal to any other kind.

There are no fossils that show any animal in a transitional state from one type of being to the next. None! According to evolutionists, changes to life-forms, by necessity, must take place over extremely long periods of time. Eons.

You would think there would be at least one fossil in the record of a fish becoming a cat or a beetle becoming a rat, but nope! No transitional animal fossils exist. This is because animals were created "after their own kind" by God, and not evolved over billions of years from a single "mutating, multiplying replicator."

Now what you may, indeed, see is adaptation, but not evolution. A horselike animal's neck may very well get longer over time to eventually become a giraffe, but the DNA of the animal is the same (the genes for neck length would be different, of course, but that is all). You see, DNA is really the smoking gun that shot evolution as a credible theory for the origin of life in any form.

DNA is a code, sequenced information. The complexities of a DNA strand are organized in such a manner that there is virtually no way life could have just sprang up from nothing. All the sequences would have had to be in place at the same time or the organism would not survive. DNA could not have randomly formed. Impossible!

DNA is as good a fingerprint of God as you can get. In fact, we only see DNA degradation in nature, not DNA addition.

Design, folks. It was designed. Any evolutionist worth his salt must know this fact about DNA. However, a great many of them still profess evolution as the "ultimate random creator." Scoff! Evolution cannot account for the origin of life on earth, and one can make a good case against its applicability in explaining the variety of life on this planet as well.

Even if all life sprang forth from a single multiplying replicator, what created the first multiplying replicator? The answer is God. He created it all. He is the Creator. Not randomness. This is why scientists cannot recreate life in a laboratory setting. Yet how many of them state conclusively randomness and evolution is how life started? Well then, recreate some, why don't you! It should be easier than randomness when you make a concerted effort, shouldn't it? Take whatever chemicals and inorganic materials you need and create some life, scientists. We are waiting!

You see, even if a theory like evolution does, in the eyes of some, seem to explain the variety of life (which I believe it does not for the reasons mentioned above), it will *never* be able to explain the origin of life on this planet. Remember, DNA! Again, evolution is the wrong tool for the job, unbelievers.

It does not matter if our universe has been around for six thousand years, six quadrillion years, or somewhere in between. The timeline is irrelevant. One day to God is as a thousand years and vice versa. The point is God *is* the Creator. It does not matter if He did it in a day or a millennium. He did it! Beware those who would try to catch you up in a game of timeline semantics when speaking on God.

Why is it so hard for agnostics to consider the existence of a Creator Entity? Is it that hard for atheists to accept? The nature of reality necessitates a Creator Entity; there are things we, as people in a system, just cannot replicate, but the unbelievers aren't the emotional, stubborn ones, are they?

According to nonbelievers, something can come from nothing without any kind of supernatural explanation, and this just cannot be true. They can say nothing relevant with regard to meaning because, according to them, life is just a coincidence.

They stumble in ascribing a clear function for morality, other than to say we form our own morals, which is a cop-out when you consider how advantageous evil is to survival; ask Darwin! I just don't understand how atheists can conclude there is no God. The facts certainly don't support such a hypothesis.

A common argument I hear unbelievers make is how can a good God allow for so much evil to take place in the world? There is a logical solution to this question, but unfortunately, I haven't heard many people give it plainly. Skipping the obvious response of satan, which is self-explanatory, the rest of the answer has to do with free will, perspective, and ownership. Simply put, there are three reasons bad things happen (remember, we are not mentioning the adversary).

The first has to do with free will or choice. If love is to exist, then there must be a choice; otherwise, it isn't really love; it's obligated slavery. I don't want to be a robot, thank you, but unfortunately, when choice is thrown into the mix, people will always choose to do the wrong thing. Thus, evil consequences are born. Think of how I habitually chose to do bath salts and how that led to my fall from grace in the army.

The second is perspective. Someone once said the worst, most horribly awful, and painful life will seem like one night in a bad hotel when compared to life eternal. When I was at the worst point with the bath salts and spice, paralyzed from paranoia, I would sit, curled up on my bed with a knife in my hands, literally watching the minutes and hours pass by on the clock. It was hell, but it is over now.

Ownership is last. This is the hardest one for people to accept, but that doesn't make it any less true. You are not your own. You are the clay. God is the potter. He will do with His creation what He will, and quite honestly, who are we to complain? I am not my own. God had purposes for my life beyond me being a drug addict. He has a purpose for your life as well.

Should we really question the existence of God because a tornado struck a town or because I couldn't control myself? No! We should mourn the dead and be thankful He created us at all! I should try to be more like what God wants me to be. So should you! There is an old Buddhist parable that goes something like this:

A shepherd was telling his friend about a time he was tending his flock when suddenly, a viper appeared under the shepherd's feet, to which his friend replied, "Wow, that was bad."

To which, the shepherd replied, "Who is to tell what is good and bad?"

The shepherd then elaborated and told his friend how the viper hissed and struck a panther also lying in wait. A panther that would have surely killed the shepherd. To which, the friend replied, "Oh wow, that's good!"

To which, the shepherd said, "Who is to tell what is good and bad?"

Then the shepherd explained how the panther, after he had been bit, ran away and mauled his son while the panther itself was dying. You know what the friend said, right? Well, the shepherd was ready.

Just as the son was mauled nearly to death, the army came marching by, looking to conscript any able-bodied young men for the war. The panther's mauling actually saved the shepherd's son from certain death on a foreign battlefield. It goes on and on with the point being, essentially, who is to say what is good and bad?

The parable makes no mention of several important points though. One point being the objective nature of the good and bad things that happen to the shepherd. It is objectively bad the panther mauled the shepherd's son, while it is objectively good the son was not conscripted into the army. The parable then muddles consequences with objectivity (or the real truth of a thing). A sneaky trick in my opinion.

Finally, the Buddhist parable fails to mention the most important thing. The answer. Who is to say what is good and bad? The answer is God. He is the Moral Lawgiver. He decides what is good and bad. (It's no surprise the Buddhist parable makes no mention of God; according to Buddhists, there is no Creator God!)

Regardless of Buddhist philosophy, whether you question God's existence because you find yourself unable to control a habit, which is bad, or you question it because of all the death and destruction in our world, which is also bad, the truth is God *is* above it all. He can and does transmute that evil garbage into good every single day. Miraculous, but it doesn't work for you if you don't believe.

The bad world/good God argument, sadly, is emotional, not logical. It has nothing to do with the truth and everything to do with some perceived slight God has against man in the eyes of the person asking the question. A classic example of an argument formed around opinions and feelings disguised as facts.

This is not to mention the illogical nature of the question that assumes the existence of evil while attempting to disprove the existence of good or an objective moral truth (i.e., God). In the parable cited above, the question repeated over and over by the shepherd is, "Who is to say what is good and bad?" This is the wrong question to ask. We know God is the answer.

Given this knowledge, I believe the "right" question then becomes: Is there really any evil in the world? Well, it depends. Aside from satan and things being objectively good or bad, if you believe, the Bible says all things will work together for your good. If you don't, well, good luck, I guess.

A common atheist tactic, rooted in the basest of human nature, is to resort to mockery and finger-pointing, making fun of the beliefs of lay people because they lack the capacity to clearly and concisely articulate and defend their belief in the divine reality. These unbelievers are featured on prominent platforms in the entertainment industry and use their spotlight to call names and incite ridicule against God and those who believe in Him. They do this because they don't have a solid argument of their own to stand on.

They turn God into a straw man with white fluffy hair who lives in the clouds. An easy target. But against the All-Powerful Creator, against Adonai Elohim Tzva'ot, they are stupefied, as if infants. If it exists in this universe, it must have been created. Logically, it doesn't get any simpler than this. Yet nonbelievers are able to turn even this simple truth into disbelief.

Can't you see? Because God chooses to veil Himself from those who refuse to believe in Him (which is all of us to some extent), and in other words, because God doesn't literally, verbally, and visually make Himself known to humanity, at the very least, the existence of God is a 50-50 chance, with most of the evidence actually pointing to the affirmative.

God, as the Creator Entity, is a required piece of the reality puzzle. Without Him, too many questions cannot be answered. I guess my point is this, do not let the nonbelievers make you feel stupid for your belief. They are the ignorant ones.

The problem is with humanity, not the world, and certainly not with God. We must acknowledge deep down there is a part of us that wants to disbelieve if we hope to get at the heart of the matter. We must examine ourselves, not blame or disavow God, in order to find the answers we seek. Rest assured, those answers are out there. However, unfortunately for nonbelievers, their worldview cannot provide them.

I think everyone has some disbelief in their hearts. Unfortunately, that disbelief, rather than being seen for what it is (our fallen nature), is all too often used to justify a disbelief in God. For me, it happens every now and then, when I wake up with utter disbelief in my heart. It often manifests in the form of a stubborn double thought, playing on repeat, running through my mind: *What if it isn't true? / It isn't true!* I can always counter that annoying little voice with a prayer and my grounded faith in God.

You know, aside from the indignation I feel when I see atheism so proudly displayed and paraded in our culture, I actually feel sorry for nonbelievers. They must be lost. I recognize firsthand the comfort I find in God during the moments my world seems to be falling apart around me.

Where do atheists find their security? Are they comforted in their belief life is meaningless? I'd say that's a pretty cold comfort. Are their minds put at ease when they consider everything in this world, according to them, is senseless? That doesn't make much sense to me. Or do they just not think about it?

When everything I know appears to be just an illusion, I find my bearings by knowing God is real and He is in control. God is my protection and my refuge. In my head, I know it's true. I know He is real. The problem isn't with my logic or thought processes. My brain isn't the issue; it's my belief. There must be something wrong with my heart.

Despite all the evidence of what I know must be true, sometimes, my heart just will not get on board. Most certainly, the problem is with my heart. Could it be I'm broken? Flawed? Is it possible my own fallen nature could be what causes my heart to be hardened? This is what the Bible says, and I tend to agree with the sentiment.

For God is apparent in everything we see in our reality. He is assuredly there, but we must first open our eyes in order to see Him. We must first believe before He will show us Himself, but when He does…you have no idea what you're in for!

I submit the disbelief I feel every now and then can be explained by my own fallen nature and ultimately defeated by the power of God in my life. Can I ask, do you ever have a problem believing? Or have you ever been frustrated with others who won't believe in the same things you believe?

If humanity can be characterized by our conflicting beliefs, can we at least agree belief, or our resistance to belief, to be more precise, is common to the human condition? I think everyone alive has felt the pain of disbelief, but without the logical assurance of God, I wonder how atheists can even cope with life.

8

Faith

Don't you know, we don't know anything? No, we know nothing. What we do is think. Everything we think we know, we really only believe. Only God knows. God only knows. You see, we cannot know anything for certain. Even if you rely solely on your senses, don't you know your senses can be deceived? Have you ever heard of a brain in a vat? Look it up real quick, if not. I'll wait.

For those of you who don't know and still didn't look it up, I will explain. Briefly, the brain in a vat is a thought experiment that presents the possibility me, you, or anyone thinking about this may actually be part of some evil scientist's experiment where he put a brain in a tub or vat and hooked up electrodes to fool the brain into thinking it's in a reality it is not. Kind of like the movie *The Matrix*.

Makes you think, doesn't it? In a way, it's similar to the Buddhist belief that reality is just an illusion. The Buddhists may very well be right. Reality may very well be an illusion. We have no way to know for sure, do we? So you see, all we really have is our belief.

The basis for our beliefs is our faith. Another word for faith is trust. The Bible says to please God, you must have faith because you must first believe He exists. How can you trust in something you don't believe exists? We all live in faith, even the nonbelievers (whether they believe it or not!). This is why what we have faith in is key. We must put our faith in the truth. We must trust in the truth.

You can throw a ball in the air and believe it will come back down again (faith in gravity), but you don't know for sure the ball will come back down again until it does. What's more is, the ball and your hand may not even exist! Still, if I had to bet, I'd bet the ball does exist, and it will come back down. I make that determination based on my experience and what I believe to be true (i.e., every ball I have ever thrown in the air has come back down, the law of gravity, we do exist!).

When I was in the army, I went to Airborne School, where they taught us how to fall out of an airplane, army-style! Before I ever went out the door the first time and every time after as a matter of fact, I had to make a conscious decision to trust in the equipment strapped to my back. I knew I could die by walking out of an airplane at one thousand feet in the air. I did it anyway.

Did I have a death wish? No. I was obligated to jump. There was no way I was going to fail the course and go back to Fort Bragg, North Carolina, Home of the Airborne, with my tail between my legs because I was too scared to jump out of a plane. And with a parachute on my back? You've got to be kidding me! No, sir, if the army went to the trouble of giving me a perfectly good parachute, why should I think twice about launching my body out of a moving airplane, roaring above the earth at a hundred miles per hour, over a "rough" landing zone? Just do it, right?

How I was able to walk out of a plane flying in the air was a matter of faith. I didn't have faith gravity wouldn't work or my fear of heights would suddenly disappear. No, I made a conscious decision to believe the parachute would operate as it was designed.

Faith was necessary in order for me to be able to exit the door and retain my sanity, but it had to be faith and trust in something real I could depend on, my equipment. How else could I justify the action of falling out of a flying plane on purpose? Though I didn't realize just how misplaced it was at the time, I did recognize the intentional decision I made to put my faith in the equipment.

Looking back, I wish I had known at the time what, or rather I should say Who, is really worthy of my faith and praise. When jumping out of a plane, however, if not trusting in God, the next best thing to trust in is the equipment. I will always remember the first time I jumped. It was one of the most exhilarating experiences of my life. I offer a challenge to you here. Be open to belief. It will change your life.

9

Occam's Razor

I'd like to conclude this first part of the book with a discussion on Occam's Razor. Occam's Razor is a problem-solving principle that states when developing a hypothesis or theory, the one with the least amount of assumptions is usually the right idea. This is different from the commonly popular definition of Occam's Razor, which falsely states the simplest explanation is usually the right one.

While simple explanations may seem the most likely, it is really the explanation that least relies on assumptions that proves to be true time and again. The important thing to know about this concept is a single fact may be used by anyone to prove or disprove almost anything, but when single facts and simple explanations are used to answer complex questions, invariably, there are other questions raised that are not so easily answered and other facts that must then be ignored in order to keep the hypothesis alive. Try to remember, it is only when the complete multitude of facts are presented, the truth of a thing begins to emerge.

Ladies and gentlemen, I propose only God ever knows the complete multitude of facts. Our perception, no matter how finely tuned, will always be as incomplete as we are mortal in this life. Just as the fish in my aquarium cannot possibly fathom the depths of my thoughts, so too are we unable to grasp the intellect of God.

No one can possibly know all the repercussions and reverberations an event or action has throughout time, except God. My point is, we must always be sure to examine ourselves for bias as much as we examine the evidence we see. We must acknowledge our own subjectivity and limitations.

A good example of this concept is a recent post I saw online that suggested Yeshua wasn't a real person and was instead a reconceptualization or copy of an ancient Egyptian sacrifice or resurrection god. This idea was clearly posted by someone with an axe to grind against Christianity and Christ Himself. The entirety of this person's argument hung on the fact Egypt had a god that shared a single quality with Yeshua.

Yes, it is a fact the Egyptians had a god which shared a quality with Yeshua, specifically the sacrifice and resurrection claim made by Christians and attributed to Him. But is this enough to wipe our Lord out of the historical record altogether? While it may seem to be a better fit Yeshua would just be a reimagining of some earlier god (that's pretty simple, right?), you would then have to dismiss all the other relevant questions and substantiating facts raised that directly point to the true historicity or existence of Christ.

One such question raised would have to do with the people who personally knew Him and were put to death for refusing to disavow Him. Who would die for someone they knew wasn't real? Plenty of people die for lies, but none of them die for a lie they know isn't true. Consider also, the number of people who personally knew Yeshua and were put to death.

Just for the sake of argument, let's say one, maybe two, people might willingly go to death for someone they knew wasn't real, if they believed strongly enough in the message, but not the numerous firsthand witnesses history proves were executed. I think all but two of the twelve original disciples were martyred, not to mention those not named. You would think at least one of them, for their own life's sake, would recant and say Yeshua was a lie. Unless they knew He was not only real, but who He claimed to be.

Another piece of evidence supporting Yeshua's realness has to do with the substance of His message. The truths He taught in the Bible are so fundamentally profound that any living person wouldn't dare pass up the credit for developing such truths in favor of perpetuating a false story about a phony deity. Especially first-century Jews, whose entire religion was centered around the fact there is only one God. A God who hates false gods, by the way.

Add to this the fact Egypt was a polytheistic society, and it only makes sense one of their gods would share a quality or two with the real, true God. In true fact, the poster of this farce was probably mistaken when he referred to the god as being Egyptian. He was most likely referring to the ancient Babylonian god, Tammuz.

When you realize religion is simply humanity's attempt to reconcile itself with a God they have rejected, then you can see how all world religions, through idolatry and polytheism, mimic but cannot replicate the one true God. Humanity is notorious for worshiping the creat*ed* instead of the Creat*or*, thereby supplanting traits of the Creator onto the created object and worshiping falsely. It's easy to see now how many assumptions must be accounted for with regard to the whole "Yeshua wasn't real" theory and how the preponderance of facts steamrolls the entire idea.

Unlike the poor, lost soul who tried to wipe Yeshua out of the history books using only a single fact about one of Egypt's false gods, I submit you will find no assumptions in the meat and potatoes of what I'm about to present and the explanation I will provide will make the most sense across the board than any other worldview which presently exists.

Of course, some assumptions are unavoidable. For example, I must assume I am *not* a brain in a vat, and other people *are* sentient. These are basic assumptions we all make and cannot be helped due to the nature of our reality (I think therefore I am, but do you?). Further, I believe this theory will successfully contain and be able to explain every other theory of philosophy, science, theology, religion, or any other conceivable worldview known to man.

I intend to try to prove beyond a reasonable doubt and hopefully irrefutably in your heart, God not only exists, but He reveals Himself to us in nearly every facet of our lives. Will you believe? Through a gained understanding of the true nature of the Tri-real Existence, you too, can begin to see your reality as it truly is.

Now it's up to you. Are you willing to believe if I present a strong enough case? Or are you unwilling to even consider the possibility? For the latter, I would stop reading now. There is nothing you can be taught.

For the former, if you are unsure if God exists, I will offer this advice before continuing. Close your eyes, bow your head, and either verbally or nonverbally ask if there be any truth to the supernatural/divine/God/universe (whatever you identify the Greater Power as), for the Power to reveal itself to you, not only as you read this book, but in your real everyday life as well. Are you still with me?

Okay, here we go.

II

The Tri-Real Existence

Therefore, go and make people from all nations into talmidim, immersing them into the reality of the Father, the Son, and the Ruach HaKodesh.
—Mattityahu 28:19

1

Protection

In the name of Yeshua HaMashiach, I pray to You, Adonai, my Lord, faithfully, and repentant of all my sins. You love me despite my imperfections, Father. You love me even though I am a sinner. This makes me despise myself for the things I do that go against Your will. The things I do that hurt You.

My sins are plentiful, God. I am full of wrath and envy, coveting other people's accomplishments. I am slothful and self-indulgent, putting my own interests and pleasure before the well-being of others, even my own family! Lord, my soul is prideful and vain. I have hurt others severely. My appetites are gluttonous. I drink and I smoke.

Yet despite all my unworthiness, Yeshua, You chose me. Heavenly Father, Most Awesome God, forever I am indebted to You. Your ways are awesome in their perfection. Sometimes, there are just no words to describe the depths of Your purposes and love. Even in the valleys, You are with me. Please don't let me forget this as I continue forward.

For the longest time, I felt kind of at a loss as to how to proceed with this book. Up until now, I used to think it was because You wanted me to rest. I had been working on the book for a few months, but then I stopped writing when my daughter was born in January 2020. I remember thinking, *God must want me to rest*, when I consciously made the decision to put off working on it until "the time is right."

Looking back, I can see just how much my family needed me then. Maybe some rest from the book was in order, but now the wheels of change have begun moving again. My mind has slowly started to return to thinking about the book, about my work for You.

Fresh ideas and connections flood my brain seemingly from out of nowhere, but when I sit down at the computer, I know what I need to write about, but there is something stopping me. Like a self-imposed writer's block. Is it not time yet? Or is it about the topic? My wife just quit her job, in part, to give me time to write. So I feel like it's now or never.

I know You don't want me to feel anxious and to trust in You, but when I sit down to write and have literally no clue what I am going to talk about, that's scary! I know this book is what I am supposed to do with my life, so what's the holdup? Why am I so unsure how to proceed?

It's like I see the big picture in my head, but when I think about the details and specifically what to literally write—it's not that there is nothing there, I know the concepts, but it's almost as if a barrier has been put up between my thoughts and my fingertips, like a screen that prevents the transfer of ideas from my brain to the computer.

Why does it feel like there is a wrench in the works, and why does it feel like I put it there myself? I would laugh at knowing it's probably some mysterious purpose on Your part, but I can't help but feel dejected, like You really don't want me to finish this book.

Am I taking the wrong tone? Am I emphasizing the wrong things? Should I bring in what I have written before? Should I just pick a route and go with it? Should I wait for a sign from You? I don't know, God! Please help me!

I do know, though, don't I? Deep down, I know what is really holding me up. It's telling them the whole truth, the ugly truth. About me. The idea of doing this is scaring me toward indecision, God. Why can't I just tell them about what You have shown me? Why does it have to be this way? Is it because I have to tell somebody? Anybody? Everybody?

I don't want this, Lord. Please don't let it be so. But I know better. I know the upcoming nastiness is necessary. You don't want it this way, and now for the first time in my life, I don't want it this way either, but it has to be this way. Actions have consequences.

God, You know I am not a good person. It doesn't matter how converted I am. I always want to follow up that statement with a hardy "but I'm trying," and I am trying, but I know it doesn't make up for what I have done.

My only hope in this life is Yeshua was/is who He says He was/is, and His death takes away my guilt. I hope in His promise more than anything else in this world, but even if Yeshua squares what I have done in Your eyes, Father, the same cannot be guaranteed for the reader.

You know what I am about to tell these people will make me look very bad. Especially during the times we are living in now. That officer was just convicted of murdering that man. If it wasn't for You, Lord, I would worry telling this story might bring me physical harm as retribution.

God, it may still happen. I may very well get threatened or hurt for what I am about to write, and the thing is, I would deserve it. Even though what I did was years ago, there are undoubtedly people who are still negatively affected. I am so eternally sorry for my sins, but I also realize sorry doesn't cut it sometimes. I want to ask for forgiveness, but I know I don't deserve it. I am not a good person.

Is this why You have prevented me from writing lately? Was it more about self-reflection than rest? Has this time not been about rest at all? Have You been preparing me to deal with the hard stuff, the uncleanness, all along? Was that what the time off was all about?

Yeshua, I feel dirty when I think about this thing I did. How can I write about it? [Have no consideration for what you write, just tell the story.] I know. God help me. What I am getting ready to tell the world, I have only recently just shared with my wife, and I did that only because I knew it had to go into this book.

I have never told a single person about the things I am going to write about, and they don't really have anything to do with my main message! That's the crazy part. My message is about reality, the true nature of reality. But it is also a confessional, so there. I must confess. It has to be done.

When my daughter was born, You forced me to start focusing on some of the bad character traits I have developed over a lifetime of selfish, egocentric behavior. My anger, specifically. No wonder You had me stop writing; I cannot build a temple with dirty hands!

Before my daughter was born, I used to get so mad over the littlest things and stay infuriated for days, sometimes as long as a week. During the year or so since she has been born, I have racked up more than my fair share of angry, shouting outbursts towards my family in front of her. Please don't let her see me as I saw my father. Don't let me scare her like that. My family doesn't deserve that kind of behavior, and neither does my little girl.

Thankfully, You have been helping me with the anger. You softened my heart, which allowed me to be able to recognize my fury, first after an eruption, then while I was exploding. Now I can see the dragon coming before it has a chance to possess me, and most of the time, I am able to take the necessary steps to slay the angry beast before it can do any irreversible damage.

Plus, things just don't seem to get me as irritated as they once did, and I definitely do not dwell on the negative emotions anymore, enjoying the rage and depression like I used to. You help me so much, God. It's because of You my eruptions are getting fewer and farther between.

So once again, thank You, sincerely, but what does my anger have to do with what I want to talk about in the book? Even the upcoming nastiness doesn't really have anything to do with my anger. You would think I would learn to trust You by now.

God. As with everything else, I find after I talk to You, the path seems clearer to me than it did before. I know what I must do. Please protect me. Thank You, Father. Patience. Perseverance. Trust. Thank You, Yeshua.

Please let me remember, Lord. Particularly for mine and my daughter's sake, you are refining me. It is painful sometimes, God, but more and more, You are giving me the patience and perspective to let the process work, to not force things. When I am patient, Lord, You never cease to amaze. The things You show me. I think have a clue, but then You always seem to blindside me with more meaning, more purpose.

There is a calm confidence that comes from letting You handle everything. Thank You. I feel rested, my mind is clear, and I am ready to proceed with my work for You. This is it. This is where the rubber meets the road.

Let me fulfill Your work for me in this life. Let me drop my ego and bare my soul. Let me tell them my evil, so Your good may be exalted. Let me show them my dirty reality, so Your ultimate truth may be revealed. In Yeshua's name, I pray. Amen.

2

Reality: Defined

Are you getting curious yet? Or am I drawing it out too much? Should I just go ahead and tell you the concepts? They are incredibly simple really, but when I have tried to explain them to my wife, she usually has trouble repeating the main themes back to me. That's a problem. Couple her difficulty comprehending with my dreams where I am literally told to make it easier to understand, and all of a sudden, this seemingly easy task just may end up being a lot more complicated than I had previously imagined.

The success of my book depends on me being able to describe these concepts in a manner any person can understand, but it's funny how apparently simple ideas prove themselves to be more complex than once thought when held under a discerning light. What are some other words or concepts like that? Reality is a good one. What about light itself? Or energy? How about life? Just a little foreshadowing for ya! Anyway, back to reality.

Reality? What does one mean by reality? I guess I could start by defining reality. For the sake of words and so that we are on the same page (literally and figuratively!), I should probably put a definition to paper, but will any definition do? Is one enough? Should I use more than one? How about three?

Any definition or definitions I use must be both quantifiable and qualifiable (measurable and meaningful). Do we really need that, though? We both know what reality is instinctively, don't we? Do you need me to tell you some website defines "reality" as "something that exists independently of all other things"? We all already know this, don't we?

How crucial is it to include another source that defines reality as "something neither derivative nor dependent but that exists necessarily"? That seems kind of redundant and derivative in and of itself to me.

For the sake of threes, would a final definition help clarify things at all? It would, of course, be of equally credible origins and would define reality as "the sum or aggregate of all which is real or existent." Come on, though, you don't actually need any of these definitions to know what I'm talking about when I say "reality," do you?

I don't think so. I think most people already know in order for something to be labeled as reality, it must "exist independently," and it must also be "necessary." I believe you already grasp what I'm talking about when I say I'm describing the entirety of reality or "everything."

I think you know to be real "reality," all things must come from it, and it must be independent. You and I know what reality is without usually taking the time to verbally acknowledge it in words. However, I'm writing a book, and I need to put things in words.

So there it is. I've spelled it out as plainly as I can. Would you agree to be acceptable as a definition it must also be testable? Let's take a rock for example. Does it meet our definition of reality? Well, it is independent, right? I mean it is just one rock by itself, so I think we can make a case for its independence.

Next, the necessity test. Is a rock necessary? Well, that's a question of meaning, isn't it, and what is meaning, but purpose? Look away, atheists! Does a rock have a purpose? Any purpose at all will do. Nothing from the nonbelievers? No surprise there. "No purpose" is not an answer, Nietzsche. Put your hand down, and pay attention!

Well, a rock is material; it has substance. It is part of the overall mass of the earth, so yes, I think a rock does have a purpose. You can choose for yourself the meaning you want to ascribe to a rock, but it has meaning nonetheless. From the sustaining of life, to building materials, to an essential part of the environment, a rock is definitely necessary.

So a rock passes the second requirement to be defined as reality. Man, this is getting scary. Could a rock really be all there is to reality? That would be a pretty short book. A rock. The end. Let's keep going.

The third test is where we see a rock, although part of reality is, in fact, not reality itself. All things do not come from a rock. A rock is not the sum or aggregate of all existence. Therefore, a rock, fortunately, does not encompass our reality. Whew, that was a close one! My family is depending on this book. I'm glad the revelation is more than a rock!

Using this testable definition of reality, we can therefore determine any person who thinks reality is just a rock, no matter how convinced they are of the truth of the matter, is mistaken. These three definitions are the standards I will use in my reasoning throughout the main body of this book. I hope you will apply the same standards when you come to your own conclusions regarding the accuracy of my claims.

So what is the secret to reality everyone has missed until now? The secret which permeates every aspect of our lives and experience and has been in front of our faces the entire time? Are you ready? Here it is: *There are three separate but interacting realities that constitute ultimate, experiential reality or everything.*

Reality, like God, man, and most everything else in His creation, is triune. Three in one. God is Holy Spirit, Son, and Father. Man is spirit, body, and soul. Reality is the *subjective/individual* (I think therefore I am), the *natural/physical* (it is therefore it exists), and the *supernatural/extraphysical* (it exists therefore it must have been created).

The proofs I have which describe the Tri-real Existence are undeniable. There is, indeed, much to explain. So where should we start? How about at the beginning? With us…

3

Subjective/Individual Reality: The Difference in Us

When I was younger, I constantly used to wonder what separated us from the animals. It certainly is not our kindness toward other living things. We are just as brutal, if not more so, but seem all too ready to throw the barbaric characteristics to the beasts. No, we are the monsters. Could it, in fact, be our barbarism that separates us from the animals? Maybe.

For years, I used to ponder this question of separation, rolling it around in my head, coming up with solutions, testing them through application, and coming up short. I thought I was close once when I considered the idea language separates us from the animals.

It wasn't long before I realized, however, language is just a form of communication, and even my dog can communicate ideas to me (like he is hungry or wants a walk). And there are many animals out there with much more complex communication capabilities than my dog. Like dolphins and elephants.

Language, as we commonly see it, is just a complex form of communication. No, it couldn't be language. So far, it looks like our violence might take the cake, but animals most certainly do not have morals. A cat will indeed kill its kittens if it feels threatened.

I think I was in the army when I discovered the correct answer—or one of them, that is. And just like the reality revelation, which is the main point of this book, the answer to the separation question was in front of me the whole time. What separates us from the animals? We do!

The thing that makes us different from the animals is the fact we consciously remove ourselves from nature and create artificial realities that separate us from said nature. It's almost like we were kicked out of the garden, if you will. We are fallen, so we create a multitude of false realities separate from natural reality. From the first city that existed outside of our native habitat to modern-day "reality" TV.

Can you think of a more apt representation of this idea than the existence of the internet, the virtual world? I mean, take me for example. I would not only escape my reality through drugs, but also through video games. I created false realities within my own false realities. I bet I'm not the only one.

Yeah, I think there is definitely something to false realties. So being outside of nature is what, or one of the things, that separates us from the animals. But what makes a person different from another person? What makes you different from me? It can't be the concept of "I," can it?

Some people think the concept of "I" is the only thing that truly unites us. We all think of "I" as the same thing, "myself," so in a world where everyone seems to always be at constant conflict, this idea seems to give some people a glimmer of hope for unity. Is it true? Are our individual identities the same?

That actually sounds kind of boring to me, everyone being the same. No, I don't think that is true at all; I think we are different. So what makes us different? What makes me different from you? Are we speaking superficially or fundamentally? Is there a difference between the two?

Could my weight separate us? I am kind of fat. What about my hair? I am going bald in front. What about my skin color? Did I just hear someone scream "white privilege"? Hold on one second, I need to go make sure my family is safe!

All those characteristics are outside things, superficial and cosmetic; I haven't even got to the inside stuff yet. I've only named a few physical traits, and already, I am seeing my identity is proving itself to be profoundly complex. So what about the inside stuff too then, like my thoughts?

I know people who I genuinely believe are not haunted with intrusive thoughts. How similar can I be to someone who can prevent their mind from imagining a wicked device during an inappropriate situation? What about the person who disagrees with you politically? Do you think his version of "I" is anywhere near what yours is?

When I think of myself, I know I seem to hold a paradoxical position of both self-love and loathing. I know many people who seem to lack all of one or the other of those qualities. Yeah, I am not so sure about the unifying concept of "I," after all.

What about "you"? Or our concept of each other, to be more precise. Do we all see each other the same? This may be closer to the truth than the whole "I" concept. There is me, and then there is everybody else.

For a while, I used to think about trying to remove all the "I" words from my vocabulary. Namely "I, me, my, mine." One can do it if one desires, but the spirit of the conversation usually remains self-centered. You see, we all care too much about ourselves, and we are all fundamentally different.

We all have an experience we call our lives. Through this experience, we form opinions based on past experiences in order to develop predictions about future events, which in turn form the beliefs we have regarding our reality. It's a natural tool for survival but brings with it some unfortunate consequences. Specifically, the problem of subjectivity.

Think of subjectivity as the barrier we all have that prevents us from attaining a true, complete understanding of anything or "objectivity." We all have ingrained biases, our subjective filter, if you will. Whether we admit it or not, all of our perceptions are flawed because of this.

Was I really being wiretapped by someone through a light bulb? Who knows! My perception of things at the time was so distorted by drugs, I cannot discern the truth of the matter. Similarly is subjectivity.

The problem of subjectivity arises when people conclude just because an individual gives meaning to something therefore no objective, or absolutely true, meaning can be found. This leads people to believe their reality is an illusion or a projection of themselves.

A good example of this is Buddhism, a religion founded by Buddha, an ancient eastern religious leader, famous for his epiphany realization that reality is an illusion. "Desire is the root of all suffering" was another one of his famous contributions to the world.

I wonder what Buddha would have thought about the statement, "Suffering causes desire." Even if Buddhists reject it, I think the concept is valid. I mean, if my breathing is being restricted, isn't my suffering casing my desire to breathe?

Buddha was born into magnificent luxury as a prince with a silver spoon in his mouth. He had to actively seek out suffering in his life to reach his epiphany realizations. I wonder how his perception might've changed if he were born a pauper or crippled. Would we even know his name or story? Probably not.

One time, I saw a video on the internet that explained the Buddhist philosophy of reality being an illusion in scientific terms. The way it works, according to the video, is whatever we see, if we look at a tree on the sidewalk, or anything else for that matter, what we are seeing is, in fact, just an optic representation of the object we are looking at. A representation put together by our complex brain using every experience we have ever had with anything which looks even remotely like the tree we are looking at now.

The video concludes all reality is therefore an illusion, which it technically is, to the person experiencing it. Another time, I saw a video of the Dalai Lama explaining how science uses all the tools of human perception to look out into space, but fails to realize there is infinite space within. In the mind. These observations are not wrong, just incomplete.

Entire religions and philosophies, complete worldviews, have been developed and are followed by countless millions of people based on the light-switch moment of realization that the entirety of their reality is an illusion. All of these religions and philosophies are technically right in some aspect, but they are also incomplete and therefore incorrect where it matters. Every day, every one of us projects a perceived reality to ourselves and to the world.

Every philosophy, religion, or worldview that places an emphasis on the self or declares reality to be only a projection of the self is limited to the subjective/individual perspective and is therefore fundamentally flawed. This is why manifesting doesn't work unless you are trying to manifest the will of God, not your own. The law of attraction is a lie!

Some of these religions acknowledge the existence of God, but any religion that fails to account for all three levels of reality is thus subject to misinterpretation by any individual's subjective reality. If your religion fails to acknowledge the existence of all three realities, it is doomed to fatal errors in its doctrines. The people following these worldviews need to turn from the tree of self-reflection and introspection and see they are, indeed, in a forest of life and reality.

I wonder what Buddha would have thought about my reality when my mind was gone after I overdosed? Do you think he would have concluded my reality was as dead as my mind? Then how could I be alive? Unless there is more to reality than the mind...

The subjective/individual reality is proof of multiple realties existing together. Do you need more proof? In a minute, I will tell you a story I think will help explain.

So what is the subjective/individual reality? The subjective/individual reality is an immaterial existence (the spirit, mind, or consciousness) contained within a physical constraint (the body, the brain, physical reality). The spirit is the individual manifestation of the self in this reality. Some people call it the mind, but as I will explain shortly, there is more to your spirit than just your mind and more to your mind than just your spirit. God manifests in this reality as the Holy Spirit.

Philosophy is the study of this reality, not psychology. Though there are subjective/individual themes involved in psychology, philosophy is the comprehensive study of this reality. Or the right philosophies, I should say. The laws of the subjective/individual reality include feelings, desires, the conscience, intuition, perception, interpretation, discernment, and others of the like. See, much more than just the mind!

The human spirit actually consists of the conscience, heart, and will. Consciousness (thinking while awake) is a predominant characteristic of this reality. As I will explain later, separating what belongs to the spirit and the soul can be tricky. If I mislabel or misidentify a trait or characteristic here or there, I hope you will blame me for not understanding rather than dismiss the truth of this book entirely. The subjective/individual reality is sub-physical, but make no mistake, even though it doesn't contain physical substance, it is just as real.

For the longest time, I had a saying that went something like "Physical reality only makes sense if it is enclosed within an extra-physical reality." Well, our physical reality can only make sense to us if we filter it through our individual perception. We can see our subjective/individual reality in our own lives and especially in the lives of others and double especially in comparison of our lives to others lives.

No two lives are the same. In fact, every individual's life is vastly different from the next, but this is no reason to deduce either your reality or mine is not real. Try to tell anyone they are not real, and you will likely get a very real response. It seems basic, but we must recognize our identity *is* real, our thoughts *are* real, however immaterial. I mean, they exist, don't they? So they are real, right?

Likewise, there are laws of the subjective/individual reality that govern it and therefore make it real. These laws are unique and exclusive to its reality. This means what natural/physical reality can do, subjective/individual reality can't, and what natural/physical reality can't do, subjective/individual reality can.

Take the placebo effect as further direct concrete evidence for the existence of the subjective/individual reality. Simply stated, the placebo effect is "a beneficial effect produced by a placebo (fake) drug or treatment, which cannot be attributed to the properties of the placebo itself, and must therefore be due to the patient's belief in the treatment or drug." The placebo effect is the direct subjective impact on physical reality through the belief or perceived reality the drug is effective. Simply believing is enough to impact the physical world!

If you still don't believe the immaterial can affect the real world, please allow me to present the Sticks and Stones Argument.

4

Sticks and Stones: The Story

There really is no other way, is there? How else am I supposed to make you see the true nature of reality if I don't show you the whole truth about my reality? Do you know what I mean? Do you want to?

I have already told you we all have our own reality, but this is only part of everything. Still, though, we each have our own reality. I have my own reality, my daughter has her own reality, someone else's daughter has her own reality. Still don't believe me? Have I not explained it well enough?

Well then, it's probably because it's going to take a story to get the full gist of what I'm trying to explain. The full impact. Before I tell the story, however, I'll put to you a question. How many definitions are there for the word "tree"? I'll give you the answer after I tell you this story. Now I'm afraid I'm going to have to show you how it is, aren't I? I can't just tell you. I don't want to tell the story. I have to. God help me.

"Sticks and stones may break my bones, but words will never hurt me." How many of us learned this saying growing up? How many of us tried to apply this saying when someone said something hurtful to us? How many of us felt the sting of falsehood when, after using this saying, we found out words do hurt?

Many of us, I do believe, learned the hard way words oftentimes hurt much more than sticks or stones ever could. The power of the word can have a very real impact on our physical reality, but how? They are just words, right? How can something as immaterial as a word possibly have an impact on our physical universe?

When I was a child, long before the influence of drugs or music or even video games could be used as a scapegoat for my behavior, when I was still in elementary school in Ludlow, Kentucky, for a string of three or four years somewhere in the middle of grade school, we used to take a yearly field trip to a little park in downtown Cincinnati. I have no idea of the name of the park or if it even still exists to this day. There is much I do not remember about this incident. I will try to tell it to the best of my recollection.

I was a bad kid. I mean really bad. I stole from my parents, lied whenever it suited me, and really cared only for myself. My little brother was worse than me. I don't tell you this to take the spotlight off myself, but to show you the kind of company I kept. He was probably a sociopath. I was doomed from the start. I was "I don't care" bad. David was "let's see how bad we can be" bad.

There is a difference. The difference is the same as someone who paints his face green with Mom's makeup to be a turtle (me), as compared to someone who dug into his diaper and smeared his feces all over the walls because he was bored (my brother). I stole my father's money to go buy candy and toys. David stole my dad's jewelry and went and hid it across town in another family's bushes. I peed in my father's shampoo bottle for reasons I can't fully explain, but I will always remember my little brother took the blame for equally mysterious purposes.

David's motto in life was "Deny until you die." He is dead now. He died from a heroin overdose in 2017. Besides my relapse and overdose a few months before his overdose and death, I had been clean from heroin for about a year and a half. I haven't touched it since. Thank God! The longest my brother was ever clean was the time he spent behind bars.

I tell you these things, not so you will forgive what I did, but so hopefully, maybe, you will understand the kind of environment in which I grew up. Every serial killer ever caught blamed his horrible upbringing for the atrocities he committed. I don't want to do that, but if I told you these things with no context whatsoever, you would surely condemn me.

My wife said it best after I told her. She said, "I wouldn't like you very much if I read what you just told me."

In order to get what I am talking about with the subjective/individual reality, you need to know just how distorted my entire reality was from the very beginning. So some preface might be in order.

I think I need to tell you about my father. Not my Father, Father, but my dad. The guy who sired me. I'll tell you my earliest memory of him. It is one of my earliest memories of all.

I couldn't have been more than two or three years old. We had already moved from Las Vegas to Northern Kentucky after my sister was born, when both of my parents were finally discharged from the air force, so I couldn't have been younger than two and a half, but I was still in a high chair, and I hadn't started kindergarten yet.

As a matter of fact, we were still in the first house we lived in after moving from Vegas. Apparently, we had stayed with my dad's parents for a few months, but my memory does not go back that far. Nope, my earliest memories of anything at all start in that old green house.

I told you our perceptions shape our reality, and I mean it. Everything we think or do is, in some way, affected by the things that have happened to us before in our lives. Take hot dogs and bologna, for example.

I hate hot dogs and bologna. I always have. For as long as I can remember. The skin grosses me out the most. I remember I would always tear the skin from around my slice of bologna or peel the meat away from the casing of the hot dog I was given to eat as a kid whenever the occasion for hot dogs or bologna happened around.

I got a lot of things from my dad, but apparently, a love for hot dogs and bologna was not one of them. My dad is a big guy. Six-foot-five, 320 pounds big. I was a small kid, like toddler small. My dad has a temper. One I seem to have been gifted with myself. The turd doesn't fall far from the butt, it seems.

The earliest memory I have of my dad, or of anything else for that matter, was when he saw me peeling my hot dog away from its casing one day while I was eating lunch with my mom in the kitchen. The mess I was making must have upset him because in an instant, he transformed into a horrible shouting beast.

He has monstrous claws and fiery eyes, and fire is coming out of his mouth as he yells at me! Or so I thought as a toddler.

Mom was quick to come to the rescue and scold him for his violent outburst, but the damage had been done. My little feet swung wildly, knocking the cold metal frame construction of the high chair, while tears ran down my face. I tried desperately to make sense of the situation, and as a three-year-old child, I knew at that moment, I would never peel the skin from my hot dog around my dad ever again.

I also learned that day my dad did not like me. Why did this man hate me? It is a thought I had for nearly thirty years. It shaped my entire childhood and early adult life. How much can my reality be like that of someone who understood inherently from their earliest childhood their father *did* love them? Not very alike at all, I think.

Going from the green house, flash forward a decade later, you can see me in my "real" childhood bedroom at my "real" childhood home. The one my mother, brother, and sister stayed in until they foreclosed on my mom and took the house away. I was in the army by then. Out of sight, out of mind, I tried to tell myself when she was being kicked out while I was deployed to Iraq. It weighed heavily on my mind though. There was nothing I could do.

I'm sorry, are you still with me? Where was I? There I am. In my old room, tweaked out on Adderall, and going through all the old family home videos not long after my dad had left. We had a family meeting and voted him out, unanimously, if my memory serves me right. I saw it as justice at the time. He was a monster.

As I rummage through the old VHS (videotape) collection, something catches my eye. Well, I'll be, a video from Christmas at the green house as us kids came to call it. I shove it into the VCR (a machine that played old recording devices called tapes, or VHS;

it's how we use to watch videos back then). Even the monsters make home movies, it seems.

The screen jerks, and a picture comes into focus. Yep, just like the label said *Christmas* (whatever year it was). Look at me, I look not happy, but entitled. The grin isn't a wholesome, happy grin. No, it's more of a "what am I getting?" grin. What's-in-it-for-me-type smile. I open a present. Oh, wow look, a trinket! Just what I have always wanted for the last few weeks. My mom says, "I love you."

I love you too, Mom!

My dad says, "I love you."

"I know," I say, and my face turns awkward. I had learned very quickly whenever my dad was around to keep what I really thought to myself. *I know…you hate me* was the entire thought I had, but I knew better than to speak my opinions around my father.

Why is that so sad for me to remember even today? I had forgotten all about the time in my childhood, which really was most of my childhood now that I think about it, when the only response I could muster any time my dad said "I love you" was "I know…" In my head, I usually finished with *…you hate me.*

He did not hate me, but he was an asshole. I am sorry for my language, but there really is no other word for it. His dad was worse to him than he was to us. He loved us, but he doesn't have God in his life, so in his eyes, because he wasn't punching us in the face like his dad used to do to him, he was being a good father.

Call it relative affection. We didn't appreciate the relativity though. It was hell for me and my brother (not so much for my sister apparently—you gotta love perspective!). Some of my dad's favorite catchphrases were, "You make me ashamed you have my last name" and "We live like garbage/trash/filth!"

These were everyday sayings in the Clifton household. I think of it as a messed-up family insignia which reads: "The Cliftons (but not us kids; we are garbage and don't deserve this last name)," right over a shield-shaped picture, in four sections, of a dirty house, a beer bottle, a pile of dog crap, and a belt hung on the wall. The Clifton Family Crest, if you will.

"I'll give you something to cry about" was one of my dad's hits. Literally.

He had a belt he used to hang on the kitchen wall for punishment. Now I am not necessarily against negative reinforcement as a learning tool, but it must be done dispassionately and on the spot. Giving in to your anger, while it may seem effective in the short-term, will only ever lead to long-term resentment and distance from your children.

When Apollo was just a puppy, the first time he went to take some food off of my plate I puffed myself up, got real big, and yelled, "No!" I wasn't mad, but I was dominating and assertive. You can portray those qualities without anger. It is possible.

I scared the daylights out of my poor puppy when I yelled at him like I did, but you know what, to this day, he will not go after unattended food. He will sit and cry all night for a piece of bread crust mistakenly left on the coffee table. He will not eat it.

That is how you do negative reinforcement, not by giving in to your anger. The whole "You're getting an ass whoopin' when we get home" will never be an effective parenting technique and quite oppositely only serves as a window of opportunity for the misbehaving child to get in as much pleasure as he can before the axe comes down.

Plus, my father enjoyed it. You can tell when someone loves their anger. I know. I relish my own enough. The turd doesn't fall far from the butthole, and I hate it. I need a break, I think...

Okay, back to the story, the first one, about the childhood field trips to Cincinnati. I remember the swing sets and fountains, the bouncy, rubber material that padded the floor beneath the scattered playground equipment. It smelled slightly like gasoline.

I knew what I was planning to do that day. I was going to try to destroy someone else's reality. I don't remember spotting her. She was the perfect target. I remember her face. She was beautiful. Innocent. I was a monster.

She didn't deserve what I was planning to do at all. I did it just to see what would happen. For no other reason than I knew I was not supposed to, I did it. She paid the price.

I couldn't have been older than seven or eight. She was probably younger, five or six. She was definitely most innocent. I was the devil. She was just playing by herself on the jungle gym. No adults were around. No other kids. No one else. Here was my chance. I looked at her and said it:

"Nigger."

She looked at me confused. I'm sure she was thinking of something less hateful at the time. What I said must have caught her off guard. I was probably smiling like a demon. Did she know the word? She must. Maybe she didn't hear me. I said it again. A little louder this time:

"Nigger."

She definitely heard me that time. I still remember the confused sadness in her sweet, beautiful, innocent, little face. What was she just thinking about? A favorite song? A cartoon she liked to watch? Not anymore. I am truly evil. Let's wipe away the confusion from her face now. Let's wreck her reality with some undeserved hatred. One more time for effect. You horrible bastard.

"Nigger."

Were there tears in her eyes? I can't even remember. My God, I'm sorry! I can't write anymore right now. I am horrible. God help me. I don't deserve Your help…

You see, we all have our own reality. For fun, I tried to destroy hers, and if she didn't already know it before, I made sure she knew at five years old. Every time she left her house, every interaction she would have with anybody ever, in the back of her mind, would be the hatred she unjustly experienced at the playground when she was only a child!

God! I'm sorry! I'm sorry! I'm sorry! I felt no hatred for that little girl because of the color of her skin, and as a matter of fact, I chose her for her innocence. She was the essence of purity. I chose to cause someone to feel hated for no reason other than to see their reaction. That makes me worse than a racist; is there even such a thing? Maybe I'm the sociopath. I am so sorry!

I know I should probably just save all the sorrys. What good can they possibly do for her? I'm ashamed of myself. I'm ashamed of the tears welling up in my eyes right now. I'm ashamed of my name! I can't help but to think of my own daughter. She is only a year old now. I cannot imagine what kind of monster would say something to demean her. Just to hurt her feelings? Just to see what happens! What kind of person am I?

You see, no matter what, I have no idea what it must be like to be a black female. No idea whatsoever! That little girl's entire reality is as different from my own self-entitled little existence as two people can get. Did I do irreparable damage to that little girl that day, or was it just Tuesday for her? I have no idea!

It kills me to think about; to think what I did to that little girl has become so ingrained into her and into our culture, it was just another day to her. My God! What am I? I need another break. When I come back, I'll move on to the answer to the tree question. Try to leave behind this unpleasantness behind.

5

Summary

My reality as an awful little kid was vastly different from that little girl's reality. A vital key to understanding the subjective/individual reality is to realize each individual projects a distinctly different subjective reality onto physical reality. This statement can ultimately be proven by understanding the answer to the question: How many definitions are there for the word "tree"?

The correct answer is there are at least as many definitions for the word "tree" as there are minds to consider the question. Were you thinking of a pine tree? What about an oak or a fig tree? Were you thinking of a family tree? Or a nation? It doesn't matter what you thought. No one is wrong.

You see, even if a mind sees a glass of water and thinks it is a tree, in that individual's mind, they are correct. You cannot be wrong in the subjective/individual reality unless you think you are, then you most surely are. Everybody's interpretation of everything is correct and right to that individual in the subjective/individual reality.

"I think therefore I am" is a philosophical idea that states because one thinks, one must exist. We must also recognize the independent realities of other people's consciousness as well. Beauty being in the eye of the beholder is a good proverb that portrays the essential truth of this reality. Belief, consciousness, conscience, music and poetry, desires, thoughts, the will, simple feelings like happiness or sadness (different from joy and despair), opinions, perception, awareness, relationships, interpretation, ideas, imagination, dreams, the mind, and discernment, among many, many others, are all characteristic traits of the subjective/individual reality.

Not all thoughts and emotions are part of this reality, however. As I will explain, the subjective/individual reality has some nearly identical traits to our third reality: the supernatural/extraphysical. Discerning what belongs where has, indeed, proved to be challenging, but I think it all fits into place in the end or mostly so, at least.

The subjective/individual reality is also what makes possible the concept of nothingness, zero (keep reading), or any other imaginary concept. If you can think it, you can be sure it is part of the subjective/individual reality. All concepts emanating from the subjective/individual reality that fail to account for the other two realities are doomed to be constrained by the limitations of its own reality.

By now, I hope you understand the subjective/individual reality is an immaterial existence (your spirit), contained within a physical constraint (your body), and studied through the discipline of philosophy. If you get this, I think you will get all the finer points of this reality. Namely, unlike physical reality, the subjective/individual reality has the power to create and destroy, chiefly through the use of the word and imagination.

Words have the power to create or destroy realities, physical and subjective. I most certainly shouldn't have destroyed that little girl's reality, and I pray, by God's grace, it didn't have such a lasting and terrible effect as I imagine.

War, peace, infatuation, and blind fury, among others, are aspects of the subjective/individual reality that are connected to the supernatural/extraphysical reality, thereby giving them the ability to create or destroy through the power of words.

How many times has a stray word caused a fight? How many times have those fights resulted in the loss of life? Too many to count! History is replete with stories of words being used to both create and destroy.

Likewise, the imagination holds nearly unparalleled creative power. No invention ever devised was done so without the creative power of the imagination first, captivating the individual, then motivating them to action, and finally resulting in a real-world, physical product.

Think also of the concept of a toy. What is a toy? Can anything be a toy? I propose that the answer to this and many other questions depends on your perspective. A discerning tool of the mind in the subjective/individual reality.

My father probably thought I was just playing with my food, and in his mind, food is not a toy. Dancing holds the same principle. Without the intent and feeling, it is just movement. It goes on and on, but I feel like I have shown repeatedly and with sound logic and evidence the points that make up my case for this reality, so why keep going?

Given the preponderance of evidence, I think any rational person would have to agree with me there exists an aspect of reality or existence that can be called the subjective/individual reality as defined by the parameters above and tested through the three definitions given at the beginning of this section (independence, necessity, sum of everything). Let's keep going!

6

Natural/Physical Reality: The Real Story

For the sake of poetic justice, and because it is my book and I can do what I want, I am going to start this next section with a story that illustrates the reality I am trying to explain. This story will describe the concept of the natural/physical reality better than I can define it plainly or at least hopefully be a little more entertaining. You will see why I put this chapter next. I deserve it...

This is another story about when I was in the army. Many of my stories in this book are from my time in the army. So I guess now would be as good a time as any to briefly discuss my complicated relationship with the military. Have you ever had a love-hate relationship? Well, this is about as good of a way as I can think of to portray my experience in the army.

I was in the army from 2004 to 2012. Eight years. I was nineteen when I joined and twenty-seven when I got out. Those are some pretty formative years. When I chose to enlist active-duty, I made the decision to be a soldier twenty-four hours a day, seven days a week. It was not just a job; it was my life (or my public life at least; we cannot forget about my secret life of drugs).

Because the military was my life, the army had an active role in teaching me many very important life lessons. Some were positive (like my time overseas), and the army was a good part of the experience. Others were not so positive, like how at the very least, the army sat back and enjoyed the show that was my tragic downfall without offering the slightest bit of sincere help. Experiences like those were, in fact, quite negative.

One of the people the army put in charge of me near the end of it all said it best. He said the army failed me. What he didn't acknowledge was there was enough failure to go around. The army failed me. I failed myself. I failed the army, and the army, in a sense, failed themselves. By not living up to their standard of caring for every soldier as if they were a part of a family. An army family, if you will.

Everything in the army, as well as life, is what you make of it though. I do not solely blame the army for what I did (though there is certainly some blame to be had on their part). I recognize I deserve the majority of the fault for my personal choices. I try not to hold any grudges either.

Regardless of how I feel about the army, I've been trying to not think about my last story. Even as I write this, I realize there is a lot of editing work to be done with that part. I just don't want to go back there anymore. It is a dirty place where the awfulness of my soul is exposed.

It makes me feel afraid, and I don't like it. I need to go somewhere I can suffer a little for what I did to that girl. For any and all who may want to see me go through some type of physical payback for what I did to such an innocent child, I pray this next story might serve as some consolation.

There is nothing that describes the real world better than when you get into a fight. Sometimes, you fight with yourself; sometimes, you fight with other people, but if you are alive in this world, I can bet you have been involved in at least one fight during your time on this planet. One of the last fights I ever got into was in basic training.

Half of basic training is the recruits threatening to fight each other. Whenever two people would get heated and start arguing, there were always two or three others who would then start instigating a fight in the laundry room, where the two parties could go in, close the doors, and settle things like men—or wannabe men, I should say. It's really more like dogs trying to figure out their hierarchy more than anything else. All bark and no bite, most of the time.

Part of making a citizen a soldier is clearing out all the self-entitled garbage that clutters the egos of the recruits who join the army to become men. There are a few ways to accomplish this goal, and many of them are employed by the drill sergeants at Fort Sill, Oklahoma, where I spent nine weeks purging my soul of anything that wasn't olive drab green.

Kids, and I do mean kids, from all walks of life, most of which can't even see another path different from their own, are thrust into tight quarters and suddenly made to try to not only get along, but actually work as a team.

Oh yeah, and don't forget the drill sergeants. They are there to help. It's not the kind of help you want, it may not be the kind of help you think you need, but it's the kind of help you are going to get. Most of the time, it is pretty effective. Hard-love-type leadership.

Everything in basic training is done on a timeline and on a quite crowded timeline at that. The army knows training. Crawl, walk, run is their philosophy. It is a pretty good one, but the army also exists in the real world where there are limitations to training time. (There are only so many hours of daylight each day, for example.) As much as the army will claim they train to standard and not time, there are certain things that certain people just cannot achieve, no matter how much time you give them.

A good example of this is basic rifle marksmanship where new soldiers learn to shoot their weapons. In basic training, the army gives new soldiers every chance in the world to qualify on their weapon without failing the course, but there are only so many hours in nine weeks. Sooner or later, the qualification test comes. If you do not hit enough targets, you fail, and if you can't shoot a weapon at least halfway decently, you cannot be in the army.

Leadership is another concept that is infinitely complex, and therefore, some of the nuances of leadership difficulties become subject to the time crunch of basic training deadlines. How do you teach rabid dogs about leadership? Well, in the army, most of the time, the way you teach anything is trial by fire. Don't get me wrong, the army will spend a million dollars and two days of training time telling me in detail not only how to go through hell, but every detail of hell, which is army-specific and relevant to the training mission.

It's like Airborne School. Two weeks long, the first week and a half is spent in classrooms and jumping out of "mock" airplanes positioned three feet off the ground. They prepare you real good and in great detail for the mission, but the mission comes nevertheless, and you can only simulate jumping out of a plane so realistically without doing it for real. Sorry for the jumping around, back to basic!

Squad leader was a made-up rank in basic training that was used to teach the recruits about leadership. The rank of squad leader carried with it no extra pay or benefits but cost more than a few of us our very real pride, dignity, and egos. The job of the squad leader was simple: whenever there was someone slacking or not doing what they were supposed to be doing, it would be up to the squad leader to step up and make sure everything got put in order. At least that's what we thought it meant to be a squad leader in basic training.

The guy the drill sergeants made squad leader right before me was Pvt. Bryant. I think he was from Louisiana, maybe. He was a tall, slender man, only older than me by a year or two if at all. His path was one I could not even see from my own walk of life. He was actually not as bad as half of the other people there.

I mean, how hard is it to just stand still and not talk? Yet no matter how many times the drill sergeants put us into formation and left us there to see how disciplined we were, there was always a good third of the recruits who smacked their gums and screwed off. Some things are just hard for some people, I guess. That is the reality of the situation.

It was probably someone from our squad talking when they were supposed to be quiet that cost Bryant his squad leader position. The drill sergeants were not stupid, and they knew what they were doing when they took away something valuable (like the squad leader rank) from someone because of the poor performance of a "teammate." It didn't matter to me why Bryant lost his squad leader rank, however. All I cared about was I became the new squad leader.

I was so proud when the drill sergeants made me squad leader right after Bryant had screwed up. And it was only a week or two before graduation. If I could hold out and keep this rank on my sleeve for a couple weeks, I could show off to my family when they came to see me officially become a soldier.

Not long after my new (fake) promotion, we were supposed to be packing our things to go somewhere (to the field probably), and Bryant was slacking. He had been in a foul mood ever since he lost the squad leader sleeve to me. No one listened to him while he was in charge, so he decided he wasn't going to listen to me when it was my turn.

A little authority goes a long way, and I thought I could wield my power just as the drill sergeants did, with reckless abandon and yelling at the person to get them to comply. If I had only been just a little aware of my actual surroundings, I would have seen lacking situational awareness is where many of the squad leaders of the past had failed.

In my head, because Bryant was falling behind, it meant my entire squad was slipping, and I wasn't about to let that happen on my watch. I yelled at Bryant to get moving. He yelled something back at me. I got offended and threatened physical violence. He stood up and did the same. I had probably threatened to fight at least five people by this point in basic training, and Bryant was surely somewhere in the same ballpark. That's all it took. Next came the jackals screaming about the laundry room. I had had enough. Maybe he had too.

We all rushed downstairs to the laundry room, where Bryant and I walked in. I knew once the doors were shut, there was no going back. *Clang!* The doors shut. It was real then. I still remember seeing the three or four bald heads, pairs of eyes and noses peeking through the window of the laundry room door.

The time for talk was over. It was time for violence. But apparently, Bryant hadn't gotten that memo. As soon as the doors shut, he started talking like he was going to continue his verbal assault of threats from upstairs. He must have been completely caught off guard by the right hook I landed on his cheek.

I went back into my fighting stance after the punch and watched his eyes get big at the realization he had just been struck. His fists went up. There we go...

I let a left fly and connected with the right side of his face, then I went back to the ready to see what would happen next.

His eyes went from wide to furious with the second punch, and he started to move forward. It was getting exciting; it was getting real. He advanced toward me. He was already down two hits to none, so maybe I thought I would try to dance around a little bit.

I don't really recall what I was thinking. Maybe I thought I was in a movie or maybe I thought Bryant would give up. It doesn't matter what I thought. I started to back up, and this next part is where I don't know if it really happened or if I made it up to save a little bit of my face that wasn't already black and blue.

What I tell people is I slipped on a puddle; it was the laundry room. I don't remember if I really slipped or not, but I will always remember what really happened next. Bryant landed one, right square in my left eye.

The visual I got when his fist connected with my face was exactly like what you see on those old violent cartoons when someone gets whacked: a jagged, star-shaped pattern in concentric levels that swelled and changed colors repeatedly. From black to red to black to red, the star grew big then left my field of vision, only to be immediately replaced with another crazy star shape that did the same thing, repeating the pattern while my eye desperately tried to understand and make sense of the trauma just inflicted upon it.

Wow, that punch was very cartoonish! I better open my eyes and get back to the fight and the real world, I thought. But when I opened my eyes, there were two Bryants! I blinked once, twice, trying to get the dual images to merge back into one coherent reality, but they just would not go together. That's when I noticed something else.

Why was I bobbing up and down so much? I could understand the blurry vision, but what about my eye was causing such a violent up-and-down motion? My knees were wobbling. I was getting ready to go down for the count.

Well, not without a fight! I threw a pathetic punch at the right-sided Bryant, but both he and the left-sided Bryant dodged my attack with ease. I think I threw one more helpless lunge before Bryant said he was done.

The look in his eyes when he called the fight wasn't pity, but he thought I was pitiful. He must have been furious he lost his rank to me for something someone else did. He didn't hit me any more than was necessary though. Bryant was a good man.

With one punch, Pvt. Bryant walked out of the laundry room the victor in that fight. When he walked out, everyone else rushed in to view the scene. Long, deep, monosyllabic shouts filled the laundry room.

I had lost my pride, ego, and the squad leader rank with one punch. I didn't hear the end of it for the rest of basic training. All this happened in the span of about fifteen minutes while the drill sergeants were out doing something (new recruits don't get much longer than a few minutes without direct supervision, for obvious reasons!)

When the drill sergeants returned, they immediately discovered what had happened. Not because anyone told on us. No, the evidence of what had happened was written all over my face. Bryant very likely broke my nose and most surely gave me one heck of a shiner on my left eye. I smelled blood for weeks afterward.

As if icing on the justice cake, in his one punch, he not only blacked my eye and broke my nose, but split the skin on my eyebrow closest to my nose on the left side of my face. That gave it away; I wasn't even able to try the whole "fell down the stairs" excuse. It was obvious.

We were both disciplined and had to scrape the wax off the drill sergeant's office floor for a week as extra duty punishment. We had a moment before we left each other's lives for good where he acknowledged he had beat the crap out of me and I did the same. Still, though, we got along for the rest of basic training.

I guess sometimes good can come from conflict. Ours was the only fight in the whole battalion that basic training cycle despite innumerable threats from other dueling recruits. I know I deserve a lot more than what I received from Bryant for the things I have done.

If it doesn't already make you feel good I got beat up, know also that Bryant was a black man. Race was never a part of our argument, but the justice does feel good though, doesn't it?

Needless to say, I lost the squad leader rank. Fighting the soldiers you are supposed to be supervising is not an authorized leadership technique in the army. I was relieved of my fake position immediately upon the drill sergeants seeing my real bloody face. No matter, the rank was of little consequence to me after the fight.

Instead of preserving my status as squad leader, for the rest of basic training, my main concern then became whether or not my face would heal completely by the time my family came to see me graduate. Even after a pummeling, I could not see what was important. I wish I could have seen at the time just how lost I was in general. It would have saved me tons of trouble in the future.

For years, I had told anyone who would listen what I learned from the fight. I told them I learned to never stop attacking once you start. What a stupid lesson to learn. The next fight I got in, I didn't even land a punch.

Maybe relentlessly attacking isn't what I should have taken away from this experience after all. I hope you take away a little bit of forgiveness for what I did, as well as an understanding the physical world is real (and painful sometimes!), but not all there is to everything. Let me explain in detail.

7

A Natural/Physical Explanation

The natural/physical reality should be the easiest reality to prove. Let's start with this: it is, therefore it exists. You are physically present in this room right now. Your hands are physically holding this book (unless you're reading an e-book, then your hands are holding a device; unless you're reading it on a stand, then you're just being difficult!). There is no denying the physical realness of either you or this book, though some will try.

Further, this reality can be qualified and quantified using our five physical senses. To prove my claim, use each of your five senses now. Go ahead, I'll wait. You see, they are there, and what you are experiencing through them is real too. Go figure!

For anyone still unsure about the "realness" of this reality, if my own bloody face wasn't proof enough, this final test should quiet any remaining skeptics. Go find a solid brick wall, or any structure will do really, as long as it is solid. Now repeatedly bash your head against said wall until you start to realize the truth of what I am saying.

This last test is painful, so be warned: only attempt if you really, really, really do not believe what I am saying. This test is foolproof, meaning everyone who takes it will pass. My point will be realized. It'll hurt, but you will understand...eventually.

The natural/physical reality is just what it sounds like. Simple, isn't it? The natural/physical reality is the natural, physical universe. Every "thing." Every person, place, space, or thing that exists does so within the natural/physical reality. Think space and matter. Think Bryant's fist and my face.

The individual self is manifested in this reality through the concept of the physical body (expressed through the seven systems, like the digestive and muscular systems, and perceiving through the five senses mentioned above). God is manifest as the Son, Yeshua, in what, in my opinion, is one of the greatest mysteries of our universe. How can Yeshua exist before everything else?

All scientific disciplines study this aspect of reality and are thus limited to error if they fail to acknowledge and account for both the subjective/individual reality as well as the final reality: the supernatural/extraphysical reality. Any religion that deifies nature (claims nature to be God—I'm looking at you, witches and Hindus!) is limited to the natural/physical perspective and therefore fundamentally flawed.

The laws of the natural/physical reality include cause and effect, physics, biochemistry, thermodynamics (or temperature), logic, the physical sciences, and so on. Note here, logic is in the natural/physical reality. This may seem counterintuitive.

One may think logic belongs to the subjective/individual, but it does not. Logic, cause and effect, and the laws of nature control the physical reality. Feelings and perspective drive the subjective. Logically, I know God must exist, but do I feel it in my heart?

All traits and characteristics of the natural/physical reality must be actions/motions, things, or measurements. For instance, whereas the subjective/individual reality of a situation where there is a disagreement between a squad leader and his squad member might be anger, the natural/physical reality of the same situation would involve my bloody face and black eye.

In a similar manner to the previous reality, the laws of the natural/physical reality are unique to its own specific characteristics. In this case, the laws of the natural/physical reality will almost certainly always pertain to space, substance, motion, or measurement. This is the box where science belongs.

The scope of science to test, repeat, qualify, and quantify are all related to the physical world. Therefore, the nature of experimentation and recreation restricts the type of results science can ever produce to the natural/physical reality only. Science will never be able to accurately measure either the subjective/individual reality or the supernatural/extraphysical reality. Stop trying to do it!

We exist in a system. You cannot create an independent system within a system. Sorry, science, it doesn't work like that. Using experimentation and recreation to try to qualify or quantify (explain or measure) either the subjective/individual or supernatural/extraphysical reality is like trying to measure water with time. It is not the right tool for the job.

The body, matter, and space are elements of this reality. Life, energy, and light, however, are not part of the physical universe, which is why science has such a hard time describing and recreating them in an "independent system."

Science could very well predict what would happen to my face when it gets punched based on a lengthy history of proven, accurate data of similar instances. Science will never be able to accurately predict how a child might internalize being humiliated and demeaned for no reason at the playground.

Some psychologists could make a range of predictions, I'm sure, but not with the same kind of accuracy a physiologist would have in predicting what happens to a face when it gets smashed in. Do you see what I am trying to explain? How science is limited to the physical world? Let's all agree, right here and now, to leave science where it belongs—in the natural universe!

Let's move next to the existence, in the physical world, of both plants and inanimate (nonliving) objects, like the rock we mentioned earlier. Both are great examples of substance without awareness. The plant is life with no consciousness. This proves two things: life is not a characteristic of the subjective/individual reality, and life can exist without consciousness.

The rock, on the other hand, provides a much sounder representation of the independence of the natural/physical reality. It's important to note here each reality can and does exist independently *and* interdependently with regard to the others. My point here is to show both how they interact together and operate independently of one another.

My final argument for the natural/physical reality relates to its inherent definition. Space must be confined. If reality were finite/only physical/limited, then there would be no concept of the infinite or infinitesimal (the eternal or the eternally small). Because of this limitation, the concept of time could not logically exist, and therefore, space would collapse as well.

8

Schrodinger's Cat

Now might be a good time to talk about a cat: Schrodinger's. Schrodinger's cat is a concept which, although devised by a scientist, clearly utilizes the subjective/individual characteristic of imagination, when positing a cat in a box, unobserved, essentially exists in both states of life and death until there is an observer there to verify its state. Schrodinger used this scenario to describe the quantum state of subatomic particles until they are observed. He was accurate in his data, but skewed in his interpretation.

What the cat theory really shows is the cat does not exist if there is not someone there to observe its state. Reality though three-fold is triune, meaning you can't have one without the other. If no one is there to observe the cat, then there is no conscious awareness aspect to the hypothetical reality, thus the whole scenario falls apart, like the reality it's proposing.

If a tree falls in the forest and no one is there to hear it, does it make a sound? No! What is a sound but a perceived audial input on the part of the one hearing? Without an eardrum there for the sound wave to crash upon, the noise of the tree falling will go out and dissipate into space, never producing an end-effect sound.

Bottom line, existence would not be possible without all its essential components. The theory is good to show the dependency each reality has on the other, while still technically being independent themselves. You can use one reality to discern the existence of another.

Be very careful though, because although you may use Schrodinger's subjective cat to see there is, indeed, another type of physical reality out there, if you try to apply the same rules and definitions to the one as the other, you may find out the new cat is no kitten at all, but indeed is a lion, and you may just get bitten.

9

Summary

The natural/physical reality consists of all space-time and matter; remember Bryant's fist. The self is manifested in this reality as the body (remember the seven systems and five senses). God is manifest in this reality as the Son. The scientific disciplines study this part of the Tri-real Existence.

All nature-based religions are limited to this reality, and so are all true sciences. I'm hesitant to even mention "soft" sciences, like sociology (clearly subjective/individual). That is why one can literally earn a doctorate in such fields based on opinions misconstrued as facts. Again, scoff!

As I will explain in detail in upcoming chapters, light, energy, and life are not part of the natural/physical reality, which is why science has such a hard time measuring, recreating, and defining these characteristics. Remember, science will never be able to measure how bad I hurt that little girl.

Just to throw this out there as well, why do we allow scientists to answer questions about things that do not pertain to their field of study or the physical universe? We get it; you don't think we are special. Go back to studying gas-spectrum readouts from space and leave the real questions to the appropriate minds.

However, the physical sciences, like all other worldviews, still have pieces of the truth. When given the right perspective and when you stop using science to try to explain nonphysical world concepts, I think you'll find it all fits into place.

Have I satisfied your requirements for believing in the natural/ physical reality? I think I've given sound reasoning for the existence of this reality. Do you? I have a scar on my left eye that testifies to this reality's realness. It will be with me for the rest of my life.

10

Natural Limitations

My leadership qualities in basic training were severely lacking and profoundly limited. I was lost and needed God. In a similar manner, through their own limitations, the laws of the natural/physical reality point to the necessary existence of a supernatural/extraphysical reality.

The first law of thermodynamics is a law that is a version of the law of conservation of energy. The law of conservation of energy states the total energy of an isolated system is constant. Energy can be transformed from one form to another, but can neither be created nor destroyed. Simply stated, you can't create anything in the natural/physical reality without the help of the subjective/individual (inventions or ideas) and/or the supernatural/extraphysical (energy or God).

The food chain is a good example of the law of conservation of energy. A plant grows from the nutrients in the soil, an animal eats the plant for food energy, a predator eats the animal for the same energy, the predator dies and decomposes into the soil, which another plant uses as nutrients for growth.

The energy is never created nor destroyed, just recycled. Logic tells us that if something exists, it must have been created. This points to a supernatural/extraphysical reality not constrained by the laws of the natural/physical universe.

Newton's first law was deceitful. It states an object at rest will tend to stay at rest, but in reality, no object is ever at rest. If you exist in the physical world, you are by definition moving. That is what temperature is: molecular motion. Show me an object at rest, and I will show you a liar or someone deceived. Even our rock, while it may seem to be motionless, has a temperature and is therefore moving on a molecular level.

You see where science is mistaken: energy is not vibrational. The vibrations scientists detect are just the impact of extraphysical energy on the physical world. Energy is the extraphysical governor that coats matter and makes movement possible in the physical world. Matter is just a physical vessel for divine energy. Matter is dead. Without life, flesh is just a corpse. Without energy, objects do not move.

Absolute zero is a concept that theorizes a temperature we cannot humanely reach, -273.15 degrees Celsius (that's -459.67 degrees Fahrenheit!). At this temperature, all molecular motion ceases to exist. No thing will ever be able to reach absolute zero.

So do you mean to tell me there is no temperature -275 degrees? It is a theoretical temperature, meaning nothing will ever be able to get that cold, but it does show us something important about reality. Namely, the physical world's limitations.

Absolute zero is the subjective/individual concept that limits the natural/physical reality and acts as the lower supernatural/extraphysical constraint on physical reality. Much like the body is the physical constraint of the spirit. This theoretical temperature represents the lower boundary to the natural/physical world where all motion stops.

The speed of light is on the other end of the spectrum. No thing will ever reach the speed of light. Why? The speed of light is equated at 186,282 miles per second. Is it not possible to go 190,000 miles per second? Then why can I imagine it? Light is extraphysical, just like life and energy. Light, as we think of it, is only part of what is called the electromagnetic spectrum.

The electromagnetic spectrum is "the range of frequencies (the spectrum) of electromagnetic radiation and their respective wavelengths and photon energies." Think magnetism, radiation, electrical fields, and light. Light (or the electromagnetic spectrum), like life and energy, has a very real impact on the physical world.

You can literally feel the warmth of light, experience the effects of radiation, and see the impact of an electrical charge on the physical world. In the same manner, you can also experience the effects of energy and life in the natural/physical world. These things are real, but they have *no substance*.

The important thing to know about the electromagnetic spectrum (and energy and life while we are at it) is that they are *not* physical. Energy, life, radiation, light, magnetism, photons—all of these things have no mass and therefore are *not* part of the physical world. You're welcome, science!

Speed, as I stated before, is always a measurement of the movement of things in the natural/physical world. You cannot move if you do not have substance (though you very well can travel, in frequencies and wavelengths, if you are extraphysical). So there you have it: the upper limitation of our physical existence.

You won't find it out in space. It is where the natural/physical world (speed of substance) comes together with the supernatural/extraphysical (light or the electromagnetic spectrum). The speed of light and absolute zero represent the supernatural/extraphysical boundaries to the natural/physical world.

From a philosophical perspective, the same criticism applies. We can deduce the errors resulting from the limitations of either a strictly materialist or subjective perspective. Form follows essence (substance follows meaning), for example.

Fredrick Nietzsche is responsible for convincing more people God doesn't exist than almost anybody, but he got it wrong. According to him, something must exist in order for it to have a meaning (essence follows form), and that meaning is solely an individual's interpretation of it (perspectivism). Do you see how he was blinded by the subjective/individual reality? I can believe all day I won the fight with Bryant (my perspective), but the objective truth of the matter is I was beaten up.

Once you come to the conclusion the meaning of everything is based solely on an individual's perspective, one is then only a hop, skip, and a jump away from concluding there is no objective purpose to anything (nihilism). The end of objectivity. God is dead, as

Nietzsche put it. But is there really no such thing as objectivity? I agree with Nietzsche that no human will ever reach objectivity, but we will also never reach absolute zero or the speed of light.

Just because we can see we all interpret things differently is no reason to deduce there can be no objective interpretation found. Isn't the fact we all perceive things differently, itself, an objective truth? We know objectivity exists because the harder we try to be objective, the closer we get to achieving it. Take a tree for example.

If I were to ask you to picture, objectively, a tree in your head, would your picture look like what I think it would? Probably not. I was thinking of a fig tree. Were you? If I told you to think of a pine tree, though, would your picture then be closer to what mine was? I think so.

With greater focused detail comes a greater understanding of objectivity. This is a truth I learned in journalism school in the army. We are taught to describe in detail, objectively, without editorializing or giving an opinion. (The journalists of today seem to have completely abandoned this rule in favor of sensationalism and propaganda. Very unfortunate.)

It is a fine line to walk, and no one will ever reach full objectivity, but if something exists, it will always have both form (substance) and essence (meaning), and that meaning will always have an objective truth at the heart of a skewed subjective individual's perception. No matter what it is we are talking about.

Nietzsche failed to see two things: one is you can have an idea without a physical manifestation of that idea (essence without form), and the second is you cannot have a physical thing that is void of its meaning, subjective and objective. Form will always have two essences, objective and subjective, and many, many subjective essences at that (remember the tree question!). You see, there is no such thing as nihilism. Nietzsche is dead!

This makes me think about the flying spaghetti monster. Atheists use the flying spaghetti monster to object to the unseen reality of God. It started as a way for nonbelievers to mock those who wanted intelligent design taught in schools next to evolution.

In a mocking tone, they demanded equal recognition for their god, the flying spaghetti monster, and their fake religion "pastafarianism." They think they are being clever when they do this, but they are not. They take the theist (people who believe in God) argument that just because you can't see it does not mean it does not exist and use it to point and laugh at believers.

Their satire is intended to point out an illogical statement: just because you can't see a flying spaghetti monster doesn't mean it does not exist. It is an obvious jab at the faith of those they argue against, but when you apply the necessity aspect of reality, the atheists become the laughingstock.

What would be the purpose of a flying spaghetti monster? To disprove the existence of God? To mock those who believe in Him? How ignorant! I know the purpose of God. He is that which makes all other things possible. He is the Law of Reality. The irony is unbelievers use a figment of their imagination, a product of the subjective/individual reality, to try to disprove the existence of the immaterial world.

What they fail to realize is you can have an idea without substance, and no object is void of its purpose or meaning. The flying spaghetti monster is pointless; therefore, it does not exist! Sorry, Nietzsche, about everything. Really. My father sucked too, but that was no reason for you to try to kill God.

Consider, finally, this central truth to the mathematical theory of probability, which essentially states nothing is impossible, only improbable. Could this be evidence for the necessary existence of a supernatural/extraphysical reality? You decide.

Furthermore, I propose the natural limitations of all physical scientific laws point to the necessary existence of a reality where the rules of the physical world do not apply. A reality where energy can be created, put into a system, and eventually destroyed.

I have literally seen astrophysicists present theories in which they presume the laws of nature "were different back then" in an attempt to try to describe the miraculous details of our universe without using a Creator Entity. Again, scoff, again! Laws do not change, scientists. I thought you would have known that.

Using the laws of science, specifically the limitations of those laws (thermodynamics, absolute zero, the speed of light), I have provided empirical evidence for the necessary existence of the supernatural/extraphysical reality. Using philosophy and reason (form and essence), I have substantially provided a compelling reason for the necessity of this reality as well.

Next, I will explain the entirety of reality or everything, using the witness model (defined ahead). I will describe, in detail the "reality of threes," which composes the Tri-real Existence. Finally, I will typify the supernatural/extraphysical reality by its characteristic traits (principalities, light/energy, life, God). If you have read this far, please keep going. We are almost done.

11

Your Will

In the name of Yeshua HaMashiach, my Lord and Savior, I pray in faith, through the power of the Ruach HaKodesh, to You, my God, Adonai Elohim. Father, I am so thankful for all of Your blessings in my life. For the little things and for the big things, thank You.

For my dog, Apollo, who kept me company during those long lonely years after the army, I thank You. For my wife's family, Lord, who accepted me into their open arms with love, thank You. For my amazing, wonderful daughter, who makes every day a joy to live, thank You, God! Most importantly, for this relationship with You, Yeshua, I am so eternally grateful.

In Your infinite wisdom and goodness, You became human to take the place of me in death. You paid the price for my imperfection, Lord, and I know there is nothing I could ever do to repay You. I know I am only saved by Your grace through my faith, but You also say faith without works is dead. I know Your commission, Yeshua. I am so grateful this book is proceeding the way it is.

For a minute there, I thought I might actually get stuck. Like done, no more book, stuck. I had wondered if maybe this was punishment for the things I have done. Like maybe You had shown me the truth of everything, but because I am so unworthy, You wouldn't allow me to benefit from the success of a book.

You always accomplish the purposes You set out to though. No eye has seen and no ear has heard the wonderful things You have prepared for those who love You. I love You. Use me, Father. Let me finish strong.

It's something I have never done before, finish strong. From high school to the army to nearly every job I have ever had, there has always been some self-inflicted wound that tarnished what would have otherwise been a good experience. But that was before I met You. Before I stopped trying myself and let You do it.

Don't get me wrong, there are still times when I feel myself putting forth an initiative. Most of the time, I actively do not want to sit down and start writing. Couple that with that feeling of not knowing what I am going to write about, and it's a miracle I make it to the keyboard at all. I do it though. I go sit down, write in my journal to "get the juices flowing," and move on to the book.

Sometimes, I am interrupted; sometimes, I am free to work for hours on end. Regardless of the time I spend working for You, the product always seems to turn out golden. This is not me tooting my own horn either. This is me objectively looking at what I see on my screen and feeling good about what I have produced. That is all You.

I can't believe when I look at what I have written sometimes. Just between me and You, I don't do much deleting at all. You know this. Most of my editing is cutting and pasting, organizing the words that have flowed through me into a structure that reads more coherently than my scattered mind spits out the material, but the material is good nonetheless. Again, credit given where credit is due. You!

Father, I hope when people walk away from reading this, they think to themselves that what I have said seems to fit too good to be a "miraculous revelation," rather than walking away scratching their heads. Really, how hard is it? We all project our own reality onto physical reality, and physical reality must, by necessity, be encompassed by an extraphysical reality.

It is so simple, Lord, sometimes I forget no one else has thought of this. I remember the goose bumps I felt when You showed me this truth. My entire reality was changed. Should I even shoot for goose bumps from them?

Lead me, God, I am getting eager to get on to the final reality. Your reality. It's where things really get interesting. As always, forever and forever, Father, Yeshua, Holy Spirit. You are triune just like I am, just like reality is, just like everything else. Thank You. Thank You. Thank You. In Yeshua's name. Amen.

12

The Supernatural/ Extraphysical Reality: Preface

This is where it all comes together. Are you ready to answer some fundamental questions about the nature of reality that have plagued mankind from the start? The supernatural/extraphysical reality is the reality that must exist in order for the other two to even be feasible.

The individual is manifest in this reality through the soul (persona, intellect, and emotions). God is manifest in this reality as the Father. Theology is the study of this reality. Again, the right theology. The characteristic traits of this reality include principalities (ethics, sins, and virtues), light (or the electromagnetic spectrum), energy, life, and omniscience, omnipotence, and omnipresence.

At this point, I think I need to take a break for a minute and let someone else explain something. His name is Undershepherd Jeffrey Mayfield. He is the leader of a congregation of true believers in Houston, Texas.

This next chapter is an excerpt from an email the Undershepherd sent to me. The subject of the email had nothing to do with what he wrote next or my book. I had asked him a question about the existence of hell and "soul sleep" (look it up!).

What he replied with, as you will soon read, was so relevant to the points I am trying to make that I had to include it. My original intent in adding his testimony was to be a sort of play on the whole "one witness" theme of my writing, juxtaposed with the witness model explained ahead. It seems like that connection may be lost on some people, so I spelled it out here. The Undershepherd puts it like this:

13

The Undershepherd's Testimony

Matt,

Over the years, I have found that a major problem with theological doctrine, for most, is the lack of witness regarding their premises. God required everything be established in the mouth of two or three witnesses to prevent these types of theological mistakes from happening. He also required a person or a doctrine cannot be a witness to itself. This witness must be independent and come from outside itself.

If you diligently seek and confirm proper biblical witnesses, it will save you many heartaches that are the results of mistruths. The witness reality is simple: the God of Scripture is also the God of nature and the God of human physiology. This means, the eternal patterns and principles proposed in Scripture will be confirmed in similar patterns and principles in nature and human physiology.

Thus, if a biblical doctrine, statement, or prophecy is actually true, there will be a corresponding parallel concept or practice or pattern in nature and in human physiology evidencing the same reality.

For example, Scripture teaches us that God is triune (a united Father, Son, and Spirit); not a trinity (three separate Gods). Human physiology teaches the same in regards to our creation. We are a triune creation (a united spirit, soul, and body), not a trinity (three separate people). Nature confirms the same truth in regards to its creation. This earth is a triune creation (a united sea, land, and air), not three separate planets. Even the most essential substance we need here to survive (water) follows the same pattern. It exists in triune form (solid, liquid, and gas).

In your study, learn these eternal patterns. There are many of them, and we have done several classes on them in the past. They will save you tons of time and keep you from theological error.

One day, we will talk about my personal testimony. I gave my life to Yeshua following a dream of Judgment Day, and there were some very interesting things taking place that Day in the dream that I didn't know were actually in Scripture. I came to realize later that they were patterns and principles people didn't teach on because it didn't fit their tradition or their narrative, but these same things were definitely backed up in nature and human physiology. Something to chew on.

14

Three Is a Godly Number

Do you have goose bumps yet? I know I do! Just wait, it gets better. Because we live in a Tri-real Existence, there are necessarily fundamental truths to each existence every concept known to man must portray.

Take for example, the three states of matter: solid, liquid, and gas. Matter, the natural/physical reality concept of substance or things, can be broken down into each reality's subsequent characteristics. Gas represents the subjective/individual reality because you can't see it, and it dissipates into the air (physical reality) that contains it. Solids represent the natural/physical world for obvious reasons (remember our rock!), and liquid has properties that can be identified with the supernatural/extraphysical world (i.e., it conforms to the shape of its container and is possible regardless of the situation).

Likewise, life, which is a supernatural/extraphysical aspect of reality, can be broken down into its tri-real description. Consciousness or awareness of the mind equals the subjective/individual. The concept of the death of the flesh pertains to physical reality (think of the old joke about death and taxes being the only sure things in this life). Finally, your actual life. That thing that separates you from your dead great-great-grandparents in their graves. Life is supernatural. Think of your immortal existence. This pertains to the supernatural/extraphysical reality of your soul.

Electricity has three characteristics also: volts, amps, and watts. I could go on all day. There are three truths that will correspond to any and everything imaginable. What can you think of? Protons, neutrons, and electrons? The 3-D world, the three primary colors (red, blue, and yellow), the three functions of math (addition/subtraction, multiplication, and division). Gold, frankincense, and myrrh? Past, present, and future?

All these concepts are proof of the Tri-real Existence. Be careful, however, not to limit your thinking to one type of reality when examining concepts, or you may end up embarrassingly mistaken. Remember Schrodinger's cat!

15

Three Common Mistakes

This is where things start to get strange for me. In this next section, I plan to show you some common mistakes people make in their deductions because they lack an awareness of the Tri-real Existence. Are you ready? This is the good stuff.

The Brain

One common mistake most people might make would be to equate the brain in the natural/physical reality to the concept of the individual mind, or consciousness, in the subjective/individual reality. This is faulty, however, for the following reasons.

The mind is a vastly complicated and complex entity. The brain, although biologically complex, is only one of many equivalent complex entities that relates to the concept of the mind in the natural/physical world. Feelings and desires are simple (though figuring them out can be tricky!); perception is reactionary. The mind is by far the most complex aspect of the subjective/individual reality.

Just as there are numerous subjective/individual realities existing in the one natural/physical world, so there are numerous, infinitely complex natural/physical systems in the natural/physical world. The true natural/physical concept relating to the mind in the natural/physical world is "complexity of systems." From DNA to chemistry to biology to the universe itself, the natural/physical world is abundant with complex systems that would be equivalent to the advanced concept of the mind.

What do you think would be the supernatural/extraphysical equivalent for the mind and systems complexity? Just something to think about! However, like the mind and the brain, the truth is not always what it seems. To further prove my argument, let's take a closer look at a concept I think needs to be reexamined: time.

Time to Be Redefined

Einstein was right when he observed that space and time are relative, but I am going to show you what he got wrong. I'm going to prove that time and space are not only relative, but indicative of two-thirds of a tri-real concept. We normally perceive time in terms of past, present, and future, or the ticking away of moments on a clock, but I propose "time," or the concept we are trying to define as time, is actually a concept called *The Eternal Now.*

1. Relative Time

This is our experience of time with the subjective/individual filter applied. This is why time seems to go by so much faster when we are having fun and drag to a crawl when we are bored or doing something we would rather not be doing. I have a story I think will illustrate my point perfectly.

I've always had a different concept of time than most people. Ever since I was a kid. I think I developed it sitting in the car to go to my granny and pa-paw's house to go swimming one summer. My father was working on gathering a harvest of grapes from a vine that grew in the narrow side yard of my childhood home, and I was impatiently waiting in the car.

"How much longer?" I asked and asked and asked.

"In a minute," was the response from my frustrated father.

In my head, I counted, *One.* There, that was a minute.

I told my dad, "It's been a minute."

"That was only a second, a minute is sixty seconds."

113

Well, maybe for you, I thought, *you're much older than I am.*

And it hit me. You see, for a one-year-old child, one year is 100 percent of his existence. For someone who is one-hundred-years-old, one year is only one-one-hundredth of their entire experience. Can you see how a minute for our one-year-old goes by a lot slower than a minute for our one-hundred-year-old?

When you start looking at time this way, you can see how the years start to speed up as you age all of the sudden, can't you? Think about a timeline starting with the child of one year and expanding out until you see our one-hundred-year-old. Now imagine that timeline going out and out and out. Past the last two hundred, one thousand…however many years you need to go back to be satisfied in your mind, until you can almost see how God, being before time existed, pops out of said timeline. He is infinite. We are limited to a perspective relative to our existence.

I am thirty-seven-years-old, an hour for me goes by a lot faster than for my seven-year-old stepson. Do you see what I am getting at? The three aspects to the subjective/individual concept of time are past (our perception of events that have occurred), the present (our interpretation of events happening now), and the future (our imagination/intuition of possible future events).

Do you see how the subjective/individual reality is all over this concept? No, the tri-real concept we are trying to define as time most certainly cannot be past, present, and future. Let's keep exploring.

2. Space-time

This is the stage, as Shakespeare might call it. The vessel. The box that allows our bodies to exist. It is physical space that allows for the ticking of seconds to pass by.

Think about it this way: Let's assume our entire reality is only the size of a square that measures three feet by three feet. Let's also assume life in this universe has a heart that beats once every second. If light in this reality also travels at one foot per second, then life could only exist in this scenario for three seconds. All the time that exists in this imaginary world is three seconds because that's all time is: the measurement of passing moments within a system.

The point is this: life can only exist within the time allowed by the physical constraints of space in the universe. Luckily, we live in a universe that is light-years across (and three-dimensional—there's your threes concept to this aspect of reality!) far longer than the lifespan of any life-form.

This is where Einstein had his breakthrough revelation, the theory of relativity. Einstein realized space (space-time) and what he thought was time (but was really "relative time") were interconnected. He missed the third part though, and in doing so, his theory is fundamentally flawed. Here is how...

3. The Eternal Now

For years, I was fascinated with the concept of eternity. It had to exist, but how? If all there was, was this physical existence, shouldn't eternity be an illogical concept? Then my mind was blown when I started thinking about the eternal quality of an instant. Think about it; how long is an instant? Could you split that time in half? And that time? And so on, forever?

Think about it this way: a single moment inherently contains within itself an eternity of smaller, more instant moments. Think of the smallest amount of time you can, and I can cut it in half—forever! Even if you said .00001 seconds, I can come back with .0000000001 seconds. Do you see? No matter how small of an amount of time you can think of, there will always be a smaller amount to be found. This is the infinitesimal. The eternally small.

This is the "eternal now." There is no such thing as past, present, and future. There is no such thing as a second, minute, or hour. There is only, and will only ever be, now! Try to take this perspective when thinking about time. Einstein was right about the relativity of time and space, but because he had a limited view of reality, his interpretation was, itself, limited and incomplete.

Freud, Another Who Got It Wrong

To end this section on threes, let's look at ourselves for a minute. Or our psyche (mental selves), to be more accurate. It contains three parts: the id, ego, and superego. The id, ego, and superego are the three distinct interacting agents in the psychic apparatus defined in Sigmund Freud's structural model of the psyche. See, I told you the mind was complex!

We all have three parts to our mental lives basically. The three agents are theoretical constructs describing the activities and interactions of the mental life of a person. In the ego psychology model of the psyche, the id is the set of uncoordinated, instinctual desires (subjective/individual), the superego plays the critical and moralizing role (supernatural/extraphysical), and the ego is the organized realistic agent that mediates between the id and superego (think logic, natural/physical).

I often imagine what would have happened to Freud if he had told Nebuchadnezzar his dream was about sex. I don't think Freud would have made it out of the palace long enough to write his paper, "The Psychology of Dreams," where he deduces all dreams by anyone, ever, were really only about the expression of sexual repression in the mind. I don't think this answer would have satisfied the Babylonian king. Thank God for Daniel!

Freud had it wrong when he said dreams were all about sex, however. What is sex but the natural/physical manifestation of the virtue of love? It's all about love. Again, we as fallen humans struggle to love the right way. Maybe this story will help explain the concept.

16

Dreamy

I'm no Albert Einstein, but I'm not stupid. I am most certainly no Dr. Martin Luther King Jr., but I do have dreams, and I'm no Sigmund Freud, but I'm pretty sure most of those dreams have little to do with sex.

I remember some of my dreams most of the time, and some of them come true occasionally. Nothing big, but I will dream of being in the water next to a shark and wake up to see a shark attack story on the news, when I still used to watch the news, that is. I don't really turn on the television much anymore.

I have been out of the army for almost ten years now, but my dreams of late have me getting ready to deploy for the third time. I hope it only means I have work to do for God. I hope it does not mean I am going to die soon.

I used to suffer hellish delusions of already being dead. I still suffer a little with delusions of grandeur. When I was in the army, I got hooked on some pretty bad drugs, which made me think people were watching me. I got off those drugs, but the feeling would not leave. In fact, it turned into a worse feeling than being watched. I started to feel judged and condemned. I was beginning to feel the supernatural weight of my sins upon my soul.

When I left the army, I was heading for trouble. I thought going back home to my family would be what my soul needed, but I learned the hard way it was just what my flesh desired. I will not go into the drug problem again. I have been there with you already. This story, although riddled with the effects of drug use, is much more evil.

I told you before I used to think I was already in hell. Every now and then, I would have a dream or a thought during the day, usually about the state of my mental well-being. Suddenly, it would be as if everything took on a sinister meaning. It would almost feel like I was trapped in one of my old video games. Very surreal. Was I losing myself in early-onset dementia? Was I becoming schizophrenic?

It would happen like an attack, usually right after I had been in deep thought about my soul. It happened a few times right after I had prayed to be shown the truth. Talk about scary! Was it an attack? I see now maybe it was the process of conviction (learning the severity of my sin). Either way, it usually came on suddenly. When it did, everything I saw or took in took on a new, sinister, hopeless meaning.

A good example of this is a time I was driving in my car with my wife, stepson, and my wife's sister. I don't know what started it, but my stepson started chanting, "Gabriel versus Ball, Gabriel verses Ball, Gabriel verses Ba'al."

I have since learned not to indulge it when it happens, but I wasn't so smart back then.

"What did you say?" I asked.

"Gabriel verses Ba'al. They are fighting."

Something comes over the radio.

"You better believe it," says the voice from the dashboard.

"Are you dying too?" my wife asked me.

It all gets too very real. Too meaningful. I realize when I come out of it, my stepson was talking about a cartoon he had seen (don't get me started on that!), the radio was trying to tell me I need their product, and my wife was talking about getting something to eat.

They are not all talking about me being dead, but it feels so real at the same time. Could it be there is an aspect to reality that encapsulates my physical reality? I think so. I think there is most definitely a supernatural reality out there. I feel like I have experienced part of it, at least. The bad part. The hell part.

I tell you this because I consider what I am going to tell you next to be the worst thing I have ever done in my entire life. Do the things I have done make me worthy of hell? I think so. I think I deserve to be punished. You can decide for yourself. Judge me if you will, but after this last one, my closet is clean of its skeletons. What about you?

There is still a lot to get to in this book, and I don't want to make you hate me too much, so maybe I will just state it bluntly. When in the throes of heroin withdrawal, I tortured a kitten. Brutus was his name. I did not break any bones, cut him, or kill him. I did not maim the poor kitten. I just squeezed him and pulled his hair hard enough to hurt him, like I was hurting.

I am truly a monster. Every ounce of my body was in physical pain. That is no excuse. I was being tortured in a state of extraphysical hell, but it was of my own doing. I know there is *no* justification whatsoever for what I did. I just wanted to transfer some pain to something else.

If calling a sweet, innocent little girl the worst possible name you can think of wasn't enough, this evil act surely qualifies me for eternal damnation. I am truly a monster. Will anyone even keep reading after this? Is this Your will, Father?

I see now I *was* on a path to hell before God saved me. You see, there are rules in life, as with everything else. Cause and effect. Actions and consequences. Either Yeshua takes away the consequences of your sins or you bear them yourself. Please lay it down at His feet. You would do it immediately, if you knew what was good for you. Either way, in the end, we all follow the rules.

17

Rules of the Road

So what are the rules of the supernatural/extraphysical reality? So far, I have spent most of my time telling you how the natural/physical world's limitations point to this reality's necessary existence and describing the "reality of threes," which corresponds to the entirety of reality or the "Tri-real Existence" as a whole. Next, I am going to dive into the specific rules of the supernatural/extraphysical road.

Principalities, Light, Energy, and Life and God

Principalities are characteristics of the supernatural/extraphysical reality identified by their interconnected relationship with the subjective/individual reality. Principalities govern purpose and prescribe meaning. Principalities include agape love (or the virtue of love-think sacrificial love or love in action), good, evil, hatred, greed, faith, hope, charity…really any sin or virtue. All morals and ethics. These are the eternal unseen things. It was honorable Bryant refused to hit me any more than was necessary. It was horrible what I said to that child!

Along with principalities, by necessity, the supernatural/extraphysical reality must have characteristics that share a relationship with the natural/physical world as well, the supernatural/extraphysical side of the natural/physical reality. These include concepts such as light (or the electromagnetic spectrum), energy, and life. I have already discussed the characteristic traits of these concepts in previous sections.

Because no amount is ever greater than the sum of its parts, if something exists in one reality, you can be sure it exists in greater scope and breadth in the next corresponding reality. How can you affect something you are in fact an effect of? Or how can an effect be greater than the cause? It can't! We are conscious. Is that an aberration, an accident? Or is it possible there is something greater than consciousness from which we came?

The laws of the supernatural/extraphysical world are unique from the other two in that they must be comprehensive and applicable to the sub-realities related to it, whereas the other two are responsible solely for governing their own existence. The supernatural/extraphysical reality governs itself and the two other sub-realities whereas the subjective/individual and natural/physical world's laws only apply to themselves. Each concept of the supernatural/extraphysical reality must correspond to the laws of the reality of which it's associated with as well as the supernatural/extraphysical reality itself.

How is this possible? Through God and His qualities: omniscience, omnipotence, and omnipresence. God is the body of each reality, the law; this is how He can be holy (separate), but all-inclusive at the same time.

Because God, the Father of the supernatural/extraphysical reality, has, Himself, three supernatural qualities, this allows for Him to do things that may seem illogical or impossible. Like creating energy and life or causing events to happen outside of time, like the creation of the universe, for example. Remember, He is the Creator Entity!

The supernatural world of God is glorious, indeed. Because we have conscious thought in the subjective/individual reality, we have literally billions of individual realities intermingling within the physical world. Following suit, what is the only thing greater than thinking?

The only thing greater than thinking is knowing! Omniscience means to know everything. It is also the law governing the supernatural/extraphysical world, which brings together the subjective law of perception and physical law of logic. It is the characteristic law of the supernatural/extraphysical reality that allows for the lower equivalent concepts of the mind in the subjective/individual reality and systems complexity in the physical world. Because God knows everything, it allows us to be able to think anything in an incredibly complex physical world!

Omnipresence, or being everywhere at the same time, is what allows the natural/physical reality to not completely disappear when there is no subjective/individual in sight. What is the only thing better than being somewhere? Being everywhere! Because God is everywhere all the time, we need not fear our reality collapsing. If a tree falls in the forest and no one is there to hear it, does it make a sound? Yes! God is everywhere all the time, so no tree falling will ever go unheard.

The existence of individual thought in one world and space in the next leads us to deduce omniscience and omnipresence must necessarily be realities of the Godhead or Father. Notice here these supernatural/extraphysical qualities are personal, like the subjective/individual reality. This is because both the subjective/individual reality and these aspects of the supernatural/extraphysical reality are encompassed within a psyche: an individual's for the subjective/individual, and God's for the supernatural/extraphysical.

Omnipotence (ultimate power) is what makes it all possible. The ability to do *anything*. Some would use this idea to propose what they see as a paradox. Namely, could God make a stone so heavy He Himself could not lift it? The answer is most surely, yes, He can do anything, but He never *would* oppose himself. So the question disintegrates.

Intellect, Emotions, and Other Inconsistencies

Of course, it is possible I may have mislabeled some characteristics. There are probably some things that I got wrong. Scratch that. There are definitely some things I got wrong. No one gets it 100 percent, right? Do they? I mean, look at the multitude of contradicting scientific theories or philosophical perspectives there are in our world.

What about all the different religions and denominations within those religions? Every single one of them is inherently flawed in one way or another. It's almost as if complete understanding, or objectivity, is out of reach for us humans. It's almost like we can't know anything for sure. Yeah, there are definitely some things I got wrong.

For instance, I heard someone say the other day that the intellect and emotions are part of the soul. I assumed they were part of the spirit. Either way, I was dumbfounded when I realized the biggest problem with the reasoning in my book may end up being its correlation and agreement with Christian theology. But even if emotions and intellect really are part of the soul instead of the spirit, I don't think that necessarily makes me wrong in the majority of my deductions.

Things like infatuation, simple happiness, or sadness, I think, may very well be part of the spirit. These are simple feelings or desires (the heart and will), not complex emotions like joy or grief. I know I previously said feelings were simple. Maybe there's a difference between feelings and emotions. I think there is a difference there.

When I got punched in the face, it hurt not only my face but my feelings as well, even though emotions and feelings are clearly part of either the spirit and/or soul. The physical world clearly has its own equivalents to happiness, like euphoria, and sadness, like pain. Maybe the solution to this problem is somewhere in there?

Another line of reasoning I developed leads me to think if emotions and intellect are not necessarily parts of the spirit, it doesn't technically disqualify them from being part of the subjective/individual reality. The three realities are triune, threefold. There are undoubtedly overlapping themes. The mind, I am pretty sure, is part of the subjective reality, though it may not be part of the spirit. Or maybe the intellect aspect of the mind exists in the soul, but most other aspects of the mind, like consciousness itself, exists in the spirit.

God is real, and He gives us proof of His truth, always *established in the mouths of at least two witnesses*. It may not be the proof you think you want, but it is the proof you are going to get. True-type proof. Undershepherd Mayfield is a very intelligent spiritual leader who I have turned to for insight during the composition of this book.

When I came to him with this problem of intellect, emotions, and the soul, he told me this:

For your review, here are the components of human existence. Spirit—the heart, will, and conscience (which reflects the operation of the Father). Soul—the persona, intellect, and emotions (which reflects the operation of the Son) and Body—the seven systems (e.g., digestive, nervous, endocrine, etc.), which reflects the operation of the Spirit.

Talk about vindication! I was literally losing sleep trying to figure out how to make the spirit, soul, and body of the person jive with the Tri-real Existence. It did not sit well with me to consider having to start shuffling themes and concepts around from one reality to the next to try to make it fit.

I forgot; they are unified. They are not separate! They are three-in-one. Believe it or not, but when Undershepherd Mayfield came back to me with the quote above, my fears were immediately put to rest. The operation of the Father is reflected in the spirit, the operation of the Son is reflected in the soul, and the operation of the Holy Spirit is reflected in the body. Talk about vindication!

From what I can see, this minor detail is the only discrepancy in my reasoning throughout this book. I had to share it in the spirit of transparency (maybe pun intended a little bit!). The meat and potatoes of what I am saying, the Tri-real Existence, I believe is still rock solid. The minor details, what belongs where, are open for debate.

Subjectivity, Objectivity, and Transcendence

Our individual lives are completely subjective. Our physical world is completely objective. Get it? Subject? Object? We are the subjects of our own lives, and the world is the object we live in. So what is the supernatural/extraphysical equivalent? How are the subjective and objective brought together in harmony? Simply stated, through transcendence. God is manifold. His truths permeate everything without contradiction. There is a deep and resounding *yes* associated with everything in our universe. Yes, all things are possible. Yes, He does exist. Yes, you are important. Do you see how this all fits into place? Do you believe yet?

18

Summary

The supernatural/extraphysical reality is where it all starts. Everything comes from it. It exists necessarily, and it is most certainly independent. You are the soul in this reality (consisting of the persona, intellect, and emotions). God is the Father. Many religions exist in this world, and although many of them deal inherently with the supernatural/extraphysical reality, there is only one religion that gets it right. Christianity. True Christianity, that is!

Christianity is the only religion which acknowledges the triune nature of reality, even if it hasn't been spelled out as such until now. Of all three Abrahamic religions, Christianity possesses the only complete and accurate theology. Judaism is true, but incomplete. A similar criticism can be applied to Islam. I hope my critique isn't so offensive as to make me worthy of dying as an infidel.

No offence intended, but from my perspective, Islam is a religion founded by one guy. One! It appropriates bits and pieces of Christianity and Judaism, but denies both the existence of satan and the Godliness of Christ. What does that sound like to you?

The Bible is 66 separate books, written by nearly 40 different authors, over a period of about 1,500 years with no contradictions! No other religion has that kind of corroboration among so many lives. This is because no other religion is true!

Jews were the original chosen people of God. They roundly rejected him, like everyone else. Islam is a religion founded a hundred years after Christ, which has no qualms making suppositions about

125

His character based on the revelations given to only one person! It makes no sense, like Mormonism. Sorry, Jews! Sorry, Muslims! Sorry, Mormons! Hey, come on over to the truth, you are so, so close!

III

Conclusion

*So God created humankind in His own image; in the image
of God He created him: male and female He created them.*
—B'resheet (Genesis) 1:27

1

Application: Where Do We Go from Here?

A necessary first step in applying the knowledge contained in this book is to recognize every interaction you have with another person is a merging of two realities. If every individual is sensitive to the fact they are, indeed, entering into another individual's universe every time they interact with another person, then understanding will be within reach in nearly all circumstances of human interaction.

Mind the plank in your own eye before trying to remove the speck from your fellow human being's. Politics, religion—everything is influenced by each of our own individual realities. If I had only had a little bit of understanding for Bryant, I might have turned the situation into a positive one, rather than a black eye for myself.

If you can accept and respect that another reality exists in another person, I think you will find much of the conflict in your life will begin to resolve itself. Always remember, however, you can only ever affect your own reality. Don't try to force your beliefs on anyone else.

Rather, with love and understanding, talk to them in a way that shows, first and foremost, you care about the person as an individual. I would give anything to be able to know that little girl was not damaged permanently by what I said. If I could, I would take it back in a heartbeat. Remember: It all starts with you!

We must also let anyone struggling with any type of mental health issue know about the truth of the Tri-real Existence. Make them aware whatever they are feeling or thinking *is* real, but only one-third of the whole truth and therefore incomplete without further clarification. Show them the complete truth!

Turn them to the God of everything. Tell them to ask Him who He thinks they are. Align our own and their thinking at the top reality and watch as all sorts of mental illnesses disappear throughout our world. Seek first His kingdom and righteousness, and all other things will be added to you. It will be an amazing thing if we all act individually and with intention to spread this good news.

Since this information was revealed to me, I have applied it to nearly every aspect of my life. I have answered some of the deepest and far-reaching theological, philosophical, and scientific questions known to man. All of which are now available to you, but there is still one more secret to be discussed: the secret of life.

The secret of life. What is it? What is the meaning of life? If you're asking yourself the meaning of life, what you are really asking is what is the meaning of your existence. Since we have discovered we live in three different existences simultaneously, what your question is really asking is, "What is the meaning of each of my three realities?"

The answer, of course, is one existence is meant to prepare you for the next. When you come to believe in Christ, I mean really believe in Him, God sends His Spirit to dwell within you—the Holy Spirit. His Spirit replaces your old spirit and starts a process of rebirth. Your mind will be renewed daily, and with new, more righteous thoughts come new, holier actions. The process of sanctification has begun!

You see, we are given the subjective/individual reality by God, so we may seek truth throughout our physical lives for ourselves. God will judge each of us according to our ways. Once you recognize the truth in this reality, you are ready for death and the afterlife.

Unfortunately, like everything else in this world, God's original intent must go through some growing pains, namely the problem of sin. I don't want to get into it too much in this book because it's not part of my main message, but it is a vital component of His message. Specifically, to repent and turn to Christ!

This book is the truth and so is He. Without Christ, I am afraid you will never be able to focus on and receive the benefits from the principles of healthy living called being in a state of blessing or alignment with the supernatural/extraphysical reality. Yeshua is the missing piece.

2

Alignment/Blessing and Misalignment/Sin

Just as no object is ever void of its meaning, so is no concept or action ever void of its *intended* meaning. Think of it like this: you have an intended purpose or virtue. When you align your thinking with the virtuous ideal, that leads to a "communion of actions," where you are doing and saying and thinking things that are in alignment with the highest reality. Kind of like how I can see my anger coming now and take the right precautions to avoid it. That in turn leads to the subjective reality of living in a state of blessing.

Virtue – Communion of Actions – Blessing

On the other end of the spectrum is the concept of being cursed or living in a state of sin. Sin is unique because as the Bible explains, there is no sin in God. This is because whereas someone aligning themselves with the highest reality focuses on reality from that perspective, someone aligning themselves in *any other* reality inherently misses the ultimate reality associated with such thinking.

They try to assign their own meaning to things and, by doing so, are making a choice to disbelieve what God has to say about the subject. I didn't care what God thought of that little girl; I was determined to demean her. It was a sin.

Money, as another example, is the root of all kinds of evil, or the love of money to be more precise. When you are focused on money as a source of value, you tend to be more drawn toward the accumulation of possessions or wealth. This, in turn, leads to the sin of greed.

Greed, like all sin, is a fabrication of the unbelieving subjective/individual mind trying to assign its own meaning to a concept. That is how God has no part in sin but is still able to be God above sin.

Misaligned Focus – Selfish Desire – Sin

Do you see how by looking for a sense of value in the physical world, an individual could technically achieve the sense of value they were looking for in the subjective, while still being ultimately misaligned with God? This is why many people often feel so empty inside, even after achieving lifelong dreams. When I was at the Pentagon, I should have been on top of the world, but I lived in a constant state of paranoia because I valued the wrong things. The heart will remain restless until it rests in God.

3

Prayer

I think it's pretty clear I am on the side of Yeshua. When I started writing this book, I thought I might try to keep my allegiance more or less hidden throughout the majority of my writing for the obvious reason I didn't want any individual reader's presuppositions about God, and especially Yeshua, to prevent them from reading long enough, I hoped, to pique their interest and show my arguments were logically sound and my evidence was factual.

If you find yourself getting hung up on anything other than the foundation of what I am trying to express (the Tri-real Existence), may I humbly suggest that might have to do with some ingrained bias within yourself. We all have strongholds in our belief system, usually the result of some kind of trauma. If you give them over to Christ, He will find and destroy them.

I have a friend whom I asked to read this book. He belongs to a particular denomination of believers. This particular denomination has some pretty strong views against some other denominations out there. I should have known better than to ask him to read it.

I thought I was going to change his world, but he dismissed my entire book because of one sentence written by the Undershepherd. Really, he dismissed it because of his own ingrained prejudices.

He did not comment on any of the substance of my book but instead chose to focus on one line written by someone who obviously believes in something different than he does. This is a perfect example of why I originally wanted to hide my allegiance to Christ. But my friend is already saved, so maybe this wasn't for him. Is it for you?

Even if it isn't for you either, I bet it is for someone out there, and quite honestly, framing this book around Yeshua, I think, was a natural device. It flows so well if I do say so myself! Either way, the veil has been torn. I will not deny Christ in any form any longer. Plus, I wanted to include a section about prayer!

Nothing, and I repeat, no thing, is more important to an individual's success than a strong and healthy prayer life. Before we begin, let's define prayer. We will call prayer "any communication done with a sincere heart, directed toward or received by God."

Many people think prayer is a component of faith. It is, but not in the way you might think. People who think prayer is a matter of feeling (faith) are the ones who usually quit praying when times get hard or the responses get less clear. It would be best for you to think of prayer as the knowledge (faith) of God. This helps you to seek prayer out as a first means of discovery for anything you do, regardless of how you may feel emotionally at the time.

I came to the knowledge of God intellectually long before I ever gave Christ my heart. I can know beyond a reasonable doubt God must exist, but whether I believe it in my heart is another matter. Consistent prayer, over time, will help with the softening of your heart—if that's what you pray for.

I always pray first thing in the morning before I do anything else. I also pray before I eat or consider a potential big decision (when I remember that is!). Likewise, I throw up little prayers throughout my day as I remember to do so. It is called praying without ceasing.

Okay, so in order to initiate a conversation with God, you must first situate your body, spirit, and soul correctly. To start with, think of a failure you recently have had. This can be anything, any sin. Any feeling of anger toward another human or a lie you told or even something big. It doesn't matter so much what it is as much as it matters you orient your heart with a recognition of your own imperfection.

Also, it helps if the sin you are confessing has something to do with the request you are going to make through the prayer. For example, if you are seeking knowledge about the truth of God in prayer, it would probably be helpful to acknowledge the times in the past when you have willfully ignored the commands of God.

When I was blocked from writing, I had to confess my anger, which allowed my hands to be clean. Do you see how this helps the communication process? Confessing our sins tells God we are willing to hear what He has to say because we realize we cannot do it on our own.

Next, think of something God recently has helped you out with for which you can be grateful. This can be anything, even you remembering to take a minute to pray. Just be thankful. I will often list the things I am thankful for, starting with the small stuff, like my dog, and going up until I am overflowing with sincere gratitude. Remember how He has helped you in the past, and He will do it again in the future.

After this, focus on sincerity of heart with regard to what you are getting ready to ask for or talk about. Think about sincere desire. Use all the desire you can muster to then make your request of God, always with an acknowledgement His will be done above yours and your will be conformed to His. Whether for knowledge or a family member's healing or even for a material request, you can be guaranteed if you pray this way and your request is in line with the will of God, He will give it to you.

Broken down, it looks this way:

- *Prayer* is the direct communication with God through the proper alignment of all three realities.
- *Humble* yourself by thinking of failure; confess your sin.
- *Gratitude*: Orient yourself toward an attitude of gratitude by thinking of past successes and answered prayers.
- *Pleading*: Orient your heart toward sincerity and the will of God.
- *Petition*: Ask away!
- Always end with: *In Yeshua's name, Amen!*

As you read and become familiar with the Bible, you can add another part, *supplication*. This is when you call on God to fulfill the promises He makes in the Bible. Things like peace of mind in the face of your toughest trials and confidence in speaking His name boldly and unafraid (and yes, even certain material things) are only a prayer away. If you know how to call on the promise, that is!

There are times, however, when words just do not cut it. In cases of extreme grief and sorrow or elated happiness and joy, sometimes you just have to let the Spirit groan for you. Wordless. Many of my prayers, during certain seasons of my life, take on this inaudible form. Regardless, they all still follow specific patterns of emotion. Namely humility followed by gratitude followed by sincere pleading. Always ending with, "In Yeshua's name. Amen."

4

Rounding Third and Heading for Home

I present this work to you with no institutional training in any philosophy, science, theology, or religion. Proof, to me at least, of a loving God. I have flown in private jets and stood in the burial chamber of the Great Pyramid of Giza. I have also overdosed from heroin on the floor of a $500/month apartment in Covington, Kentucky. They say in your thirties, you develop your worldview. I think God gave me this insight.

The same God who made this universe out of nothing would easily devote Himself to you entirely if you would only let Him. This is the same God who manifested Himself and conquered death on our behalf. Using the Tri-real Existence as proof, many questions have been explained. It's now up to you to apply the concepts you have learned.

Take for example, the Holy Trinity, a concept that has stumped theologians since its recognition. As explained previously, this tricky theological concept easily clicks into place when you understand God is triune and manifests in each of the three realities as Father in the supernatural/extraphysical, Son in the natural/physical world, and Holy Spirit in the subjective/individual reality. Triune, not trinitarian. Goose bump stuff?

How about the image and likeness question, which essentially asks how are we, as humans, actually made in the image and likeness of God? This concept, however, also earlier explained, easily fits when you compare the spirit, body, and soul aspect of humans to the Holy Spirit, Son, and Father aspect of our triune God.

Which brings me, finally, to the last thing separating us from the animals. You got it! It is our image and likeness. You may think animals lack souls, but I don't think that is completely true. I propose animals lack the subjective/individual component to reality; they have no mind. At least not one that questions its existence like we do. They have no knowledge of good and evil. They never partook of the fruit. In turn, our physical bodies are what separates us from the angels.

You see, there is no other creation like us. We are special. Don't believe the astrophysicist. Because even if there are an infinite number of parallel universes out there, that does not diminish how God is. We and our reality may very well be triune, but I believe God may, in fact, be *infiune* (that is infinitely unified—huh, new word!). So for the blob creatures of parallel reality number 468, God is also as unified to them as He is to us. However, these are thoughts for another time—and place!

At this point, I have called on you to search your own heart more times than I probably should have. If you have read this far, I have faith I needn't have begged you to read to begin with. If you haven't, then this part isn't for you, anyways.

Have the things I've said made sense? Do you think it might possibly just be a figment of my imagination? I propose this theory of thought is the one and only truth with regard to how to think about reality correctly. Try it for yourself, and please, if you found this book thought-provoking or hopefully life-changing, consider purchasing a few copies for those you care about.

My daughter is fifteen months old now, and I would like to provide her with as good a life as I can. Like everything else, though, it is ultimately up to God, in whom I have all the faith in the world. Into what do you put your faith? Is it real?

5

The Hardest Thing to Consider

Throughout this book, I have presented quite a few concepts. Most of which, I am willing to bet, if not new to you, were at least shown to you under a new light. I hope you come away from this feeling like you "get" what I'm talking about. I think most people who actually read this book in its entirety will get what I am talking about. I think it makes too much sense for people not to get it.

I mean, come on, we have all heard the sayings, "Whatever floats your boat" and "To each his own." Yeah, I think we all instinctively understand the subjective/individual concept. The Bible says God wrote His law on your heart. Is that relevant to this?

Likewise, I think everyone reading this has been physically hurt before. If not in a fistfight, where getting punched in the face served as transcendental justice for a past sin, then when you have fallen down and scraped your knee as kid. It has happened to nearly everyone; I am willing to bet.

In the end, it all comes down to belief. Is it so hard to believe we were created? I believe most people in this world still believe in the supernatural. I have given you evidence for the extraphysical as well.

So there you have it. I hope I explained it clearly. If I did, then you should have no problem understanding what I am saying. Life, subjectivity, the physical world, the supernatural world…God. Are these things hard for you to believe in? I hope not anymore, but what about the One who matters most? What about Yeshua?

I had originally thought I would not put a Yeshua chapter in this book because my conversion story is so unappealing, and I happen to exist outside the norm of even most Christians. There are things about me most people would probably find very un-Christ-like, and that others would say make me unable to be a Christian altogether!

I still smoke weed, for example. I know, I know, trust me, I know, but that's all I do anymore. I don't even drink regularly, praise Yeshua! I do not want to condone it in any way because at the very least, smoking is a sin against my own flesh, but it *is* just a plant, with minimal mind-altering effects (at least the effects are minimal to me after smoking for twenty-plus years).

My wife said it best, and the Bible tends to back up her sentiment. She says, "It's what you do with it that matters." Meaning how bad can weed really be if, along with getting high, I am kind to my family, read the Bible, and meditate on His Word constantly? Not that bad at all, I think.

The Bible says something similar (though they were talking directly about food, I would challenge you to seek other applications). The Bible says it isn't what a person puts into them that defiles them, it is what comes out of them that defiles. For out of the heart comes murder, adultery, and all other kinds of uncleanness. I would caution the reader here; do not be like the Pharisees of old, who were well-known for their ceremonial washing of cups and pots and hands and equally infamous for their hard-heartedness toward God and His Real Rules.

In actuality, smoking weed does not defile my soul. It just helps me to relax and detach from this fake society that is constantly trying to envelop me. I want to go back to the garden, please! Can it be all bad to escape a reality that is, itself, counterfeit? Again, I think not.

There was a little rant I had originally wanted to put here to illustrate my point, but my wife and a good friend told me to take it out. Suffice it to say, I believe this world is evil, and it is trying to drive people insane with ridiculous rules and phony hysteria. What is even crazier is many people don't even seem to care! This world is losing its mind.

Regardless of this evil world and how it is trying to pacify and subdue people, I know I should probably stop smoking marijuana. It can't be a good testament to God that I am a stoner, but then again, maybe that's how His Holy Power will show through perfectly. Through my imperfection.

I have asked God to help me quit more times than you can imagine. I am not giving myself a pass, but He seems to be more focused on my character than anything else. My anger still needs constant attention, and I feel like He is telling me to start loving more.

Hopefully, I will quit one day, but not today and probably not tomorrow. Until then it will be caffeine, sugar, and THC only. That's it for me, thank you, please!

In a similar manner, my distrust for medical science tends to isolate me from not only society, but the majority of Christians. For example, I do not believe in vaccines. What I mean by saying this is vaccines may very well be effective in preventing whatever malady they are designed to counter and only slightly effective for some, like the flu vaccine. You mean to tell me you gotta take it every year? What kind of vaccine is that? I'm tired of scoffing!

Regardless of the effectiveness of vaccines, there are undoubtedly side effects (either wholly unreported or at the very least underreported), which the medical community will not research. They hide behind the statement, "There is no body of research to suggest any link between vaccines and autism or other neurological disorders." Well, that's because no one will do the stupid research! They won't even fund it! Why do you think that is?

I'm not here to convince you of anything regarding vaccines. Just know I am not in favor of them, especially not when administered at birth. If you want to, please do. Get any and every vaccine medical science develops.

My stepmother recently had a stroke less than a month after getting a newly developed vaccine. Neither she nor my dad nor the doctors who treated her seem to think or even care if the vaccine caused the stroke. The doctors actually told my dad it was probably him doing too much for my stepmother that caused it. There was no discussion about whether or not it may have been the shot. (See what I mean about refusing to research?! It extends beyond the laboratory and university; their neglect is systemic.)

In my opinion, way too many people put way too much faith into not only medical science (it is and will only ever be a body of research, that's it!), but the opinion of a doctor. Just because they went to medical school! Not me, though. Keep your dead animal cells, mercury, and aluminum nanoparticles away from me and my child please!

Doctrinally, there are still other things that separate me from the pack. I observe the Sabbath on Saturday because it's the day God said it should be, as a permanent statute…forever. Sorry, majority of the western Christian world. Hey, to each his own, right?

I don't eat pork because, well, it is a sacrifice that I can make (since I apparently cannot stop smoking weed!). I know all things are clean; but I'm telling you, at least three times in a row, when I was battling with my conscience on whether or not it was okay to eat pork, God told me not to. Miraculous? No, but I try to go with His flow, not against it. So no pork. It is a sincere sacrifice I make for God. I love bacon, but I love Yeshua even more!

Speaking of Yeshua, I call Him Yeshua, not Jesus, because Yeshua is His name. Why pronounce it differently? I understand transliteration, but why would you transliterate someone's name without paying any attention to the correct pronunciation? To me, it seems like a silly oversight.

I don't blame anyone for calling Him Jesus. I still do it myself from time to time, but it doesn't make sense to me. Call Him what He is called. Why the intentional confusion? I don't get it. You see, all these things, and more, usually cause me to be set apart.

I really am kind of a lone-wolf Christian, though some would suggest there can be no such thing. I like to think of it as being a sheep in wolves' clothing, if you will. I have always been sincere in my search though. No one can take that away from me.

In all actuality, it was probably my sincerity that caused me to have to leave the group to begin with. All institutions of man are flawed, especially in the church. I was looking for perfection. I was looking for the Truth. Because of my sincerity, I can give a reasoned explanation for everything I believe in.

When I first came to an intellectual understanding about the necessity of a Creator Entity (i.e., God), I was still a long way from accepting Christ into my heart. I was eager to absorb any sound theology from any source I could find and found plenty of sound theology in the Christian faith. However, I would not even consider the possibility the Bible might be true or Yeshua might be who He says He is.

I knew God must exist long before I ever felt not only love for Him, but true repentance in my heart for the ways I have dishonored Him in the past. Like so many people, I believed for the longest time me and God were "cool." I didn't need Yeshua. God got me, and I got Him. I have friends like that even still, though our friendships are not what they used to be.

They know in their hearts the Bible is a lie and Yeshua is not God. They know nothing. They don't even believe to begin with. They disbelieve. In Yeshua. Their hearts are stony toward Him because they "know better."

I think most of our culture has been scandalized by the name of Yeshua. Meaning any and every slanderous thing you could say about a person has been, and is currently in vogue of being, said about Yeshua. Remember the whole "He isn't real" argument from the beginning?

No one else in history has been so maligned as Christ. It's no wonder people who don't sincerely search for Him don't find Him. Yet there He is. Everyone, and I mean everyone, has heard about Yeshua (or Jesus at least!). So what's your excuse?

I really hope you are not against Christianity because of the way it has been exploited and abused by people in the past. If you are the personal victim of deceitful, fake Christians and their practices, I, here and now, personally apologize for the ways evil people have tried to corrupt God's message and spiritually abuse those who needed help. They will pay the price for their deeds. Please do not let their lies tarnish the Truth.

Ravi Zacharias was an extremely intelligent Christian apologist who had a way with words. He put it this way. He said to be careful never to judge a philosophy or worldview by the way people have abused it in the past. Every religion's history has its dark moments, and every doctrine ever devised is able to be manipulated by those who would desire to distort and corrupt the Truth of God for their own personal gain and power.

Though I never sought to falsely lead people for my own gain, before Yeshua saved me, I was no better than the antichrists. For as long as I can remember, I knew I was no good. Before I even came to understand the necessity of God, back when I tried to kill myself in high school, I knew I was doomed.

Perfectionism disorder is what the doctors called it. The scars on my wrist tell the tale. I held everything to too high of a standard, apparently. Even myself. You see, deep down, I have always known I needed to be saved; I couldn't do it on my own. That has always been part of my fundamental worldview, even before I recognized it as such. If it is not part of yours, I don't know what to tell you.

Like most of my friends though, I also knew Yeshua was *not* the answer. How could He be? Pick any defect you want, and there is someone out there shouting He has it. How can three Gods be one? How can a virgin give birth? No one rises from the dead!

Pick any perceived illogical paradox you want and apply it to Yeshua; you will find plenty of company. That's what I mean by scandalized. Ravi Zacharias said it best. He said, "Anyone can make any worldview look dumb." I had sincerely hoped to be able to give Mr. Zacharias a copy of my book before he died, but I was not.

For me, it just happened one day. Nothing miraculous or noteworthy. I was just sitting in my car, driving a package from one place to the next, as I was wont to do because of my courier job, when it hit me. It just made sense.

I always knew I had to be saved. I also "knew" Yeshua wasn't the answer, but you know what the Bible says? It was written nearly two thousand years ago, but it is just as true today as it was back then. It says no other name has been given under heaven by which men must be saved.

That means there is no cult of Matthew or religion of Danielle that says your sins can be forgiven through the work of anyone other than Jesus (or Yeshua)! Even a religion like Mormonism is forced to concede the savior aspect of their theology to Christ, not Joseph Smith or some imaginary figure from ancient America.

I think that's a miracle, don't you? I mean, really, in two thousand years, no one else has come along with a similar message to Yeshua? At least not anyone who has stuck around for long. Doesn't that say something to you? It did to me that day.

There was nothing special about the day, and in fact, I had been praying for God to show me the truth of Yeshua for a few years—if there was any truth to be had, that is. No sign from God, so I took it as a sign. Then one day, in my car, just thinking about life and stuff, it made sense. I knew I needed to be saved, and I knew I couldn't do it myself.

There was no one else in the history of the universe by which anyone says someone can be saved. All other world religions that even speak on salvation claim you can do it on your own, like Judaism and Islam. Keep trying to rely solely on your own ability to follow God's Law, and you will never succeed, Jews and Muslims! We need to be saved, I needed to be saved, and God loves us. I knew God loved me. So He would save me, wouldn't He?

All of the sudden, it just made sense. Yeshua had to be real! For the first time in my life, I found myself thinking of the ways it was right, rather than imagining a million different ways it could be wrong. That day, for the first time, Yeshua no longer looked dumb to me. On the spot, I prayed to Him, for real, for the first time in my life, and I have never looked back.

The incident in my car happened in early 2019, April or May. Today is July 30, 2021. I gave my life to Christ, and in under three years, I had a revelation and wrote a book that I believe should change the world. What might He give you if you came to Him with similar contrition?

I had sincerely hoped to be able to give Mr. Zacharias a copy of this book before he died. I had been listening to his fifteen-minute daily radio program called *Just Thinking* ever since I found it on the radio, in my car, while I worked. That I am not able to send him a copy of this book is a regret I will have until I see him on the other side.

When I received the idea for the Tri-real Existence, I used to fantasize about walking up to him, dropping my book into his lap, and saying, "I think you have been looking for this." Melodramatic? I know. That's why it was a fantasy, I guess.

Now, it's time for my final challenge to you. Most of you, sadly, will not accept it. It is to believe in Yeshua HaMashiach, Jesus Christ, with all your body, mind, and soul. For those who do accept this last and hardest challenge, be prepared, even when you choose Christ, choosing to love him completely will cost you everything you have. It will take you the rest of your life. You have no idea what you will receive in return.

I mean, hey, look what He did for me! I am a drug-addled nobody making claims that refute some of the smartest intellects in human history. Newton, Nietzsche, Freud, Einstein. Either God is real and has inspired my soul or maybe I really am a brain in a vat!

I will say this world has taken on an eerily strange, unreal feeling since I have finished this book. Don't worry though, I'm not going to have a mental breakdown (again, sorry, Nietzsche). I know this world is *not* real. The next one is.

I hope with all my faith I will make it to the next world. I believe I will because of Yeshua and what He did for me. I pray you will find me there and tell me I had an impact on your practice life, like I plan to do with Mr. Zacharias. It will make me feel good.

6

The End, Really

In the name of Yeshua HaMashiach, my Lord, my Savior, my Friend, I pray in faith to You, the One and Only God of the Universe, Adonai Elohim Tzva'ot, through the power of Your Comforter, the Ruach HaKodesh, which dwells within me.

Father, I cannot believe I have done this! I finished a book! I know I shouldn't use exclamations so much, but it feels appropriate! I love You so much! Thank You! Thank You! Thank You! I know there is no way I can ever repay You, so thank You!

I don't care if someone thinks this book is too Jesus-y. I don't care if I get threatened because of what I wrote in it or because of my allegiance to You. I don't care! You are all I care about, and because I care about You, everything else in my life has fallen into its proper place.

I thought this book might take me years or even a lifetime to finish, but You have other plans apparently. Under two years, wow! From November 2019 until today, July 30, 2021. Not long at all, and I took a year off in the middle for my daughter!

Father, I know this book should change the world. I also realize it may very well fall on deaf ears. Like so much of Your truth, it may very well "fall as water on a stone." This is not what matters though. I did it. That matters. I am boldly proclaiming Your message! I know You will provide for me all the way, regardless of the success of this book.

I told my wife I would get a job as soon as I finished writing, and even if this book is not read by another soul, I know I will find purpose for my life in the daily interactions You prepare for me. Lord, Your word does not return void, but always accomplishes what it sets out to.

I hope I have done good for You, Yeshua. You are, indeed, helping me grow into a better person. Up until now, my life has not been filled with many great works, and I am quite introverted. This is what I have though. Until the day I am perfected in You, everything I am is in it. With infinite gratitude and love. It is all for You.

And you.

Amen.

Now go read the Bible!

Addendum

Numerology

I put this next section of the book as an addendum because math is boring to most people, and I am hoping you were more or less enthralled with my book without being subjected to an amateur math lesson. Regardless, this is what I intend to present as mathematical evidence for the Tri-real Existence.

1. The Three Functions of Math and How They Relate to the Tri-Real Existence

Just as there are three truths associated with every concept imaginable, numbers and math are no exception. We previously mentioned the three functions of math. Think that's a coincidence? I don't believe in coincidences anymore. Here is math explained.

2. Division, Addition/Subtraction, and Multiplication

In the real world, division is impossible; you can't take apart something without deconstructing its reality as a whole into a subjective interpretation of the pieces of that whole. For instance, if you have an apple, you can add an apple to that one and take it away, but you cannot get more apples by dividing the one you have. Think reflection, insight, introspection equivalents.

Thus, while division is the subjective/individual equivalent to math, so is addition and subtraction the reflection of the natural/physical world in math. Multiplication is the supernatural/extraphysical side of math. In the same way you cannot divide an apple to get more apples, you cannot multiply any number of apples you have through merely physical means. For example, you cannot take three apples, do something with another three apples, and end up with nine apples.

Multiplication is a function of math where normal logic doesn't exist, and you really can make nine apples from three and three. Another proof of the existence of the supernatural/extraphysical? You decide.

3. Numbers Redefined

I think we have established because of a lack of awareness of the Tri-real Existence all theories, concepts, and definitions established by man thus far have at least been misinterpreted, and at the most wholly ignorant of at least one major aspect of reality, it is necessary to put a fresh set of eyes on the theory of numbers. My number theory begins with 0.

4. Let's Start with 0: The Fake Number

Let me tell you a little bit about an idea. Nothing, really. Really, nothing. The idea is the concept of nothingness. How can you have zero of anything in a physical world? In fact, how can zero even exist in a physical world? The answer is that it can't. Zero is the subjective/individual reality's concept of nothing having a physical world impact by the creation of, not only a number, but a concept.

Proof. In order for any number to be considered real, it must satisfy the three functions of math. Namely addition/subtraction, multiplication, and division.

If you take any number and divide, multiply, subtract, or add it to any other number, you should get a real answer. Not the case with zero. For instance:

$3+1=4$ $1+3=4$
$1\times3=3$ $3\times1=3$
$3/1=3$ $1/3=0.3$ (repeating)

Now let's try that with zero:

$0+1=1$ $1+0=1$

$0 \times 1 = 0$ $1 \times 0 = 0$

$0/1 = 0$ But $1/0 = $ Error?

How can that be? Don't believe me; go ahead and try it for yourself!

I think you'll find my explanation fits the best. It's not original either. The concept of 0 as a number didn't gain prominence until the sixth century BCE! That's about three thousand years of recorded human history with *no* zero! Ancient people inherently saw the logical fallacy of trying to represent nothingness with numbers. If you have no apples, you do not have any apples; you do not have zero apples.

Imaginary numbers = 0

I doubt any mathematician will take what I have written seriously, but from my perspective, the only thing wrong with eliminating zero as a number would be its ruination of our ten-digit number system. As I was reminded the other day, it is because of zero that we are able to literally count forever. Rather, I should say, it's because we put zero on the end of real numbers (like 1 turning into 10 when you put a zero behind it, or 2 and 20, and 3 and 30, ad infinitum). But getting rid of zero as a number doesn't necessarily have to end our counting by tens. Just start from one and go to 10, like you do on your fingers.

That is the first set of 10. It is 1 through 10. It is not 0 through 9. Make sense? Whereas the old ten-digit number system would go: 0, 1, 2, 3, 4, 5, 6, 7, 8, 9, with the next sequence starting at 10 and going through 19 (then 20 through 29, 30 through 39, ad infinitum), the new system would start where it belongs, with 1, followed by 2, 3, 4, 5, 6, 7, 8, 9, 10 (then 11 through 20, 21 through 30, 31 through 40, ad infinitum. Forever!).

Going backward from one, there should be a mathematical symbol representing "nothing" or nothingness. If you can acknowledge the non-number aspect of this symbol, it might as well stay at zero or 0. If you can't get there mentally, I suggest a dot or filled-in circle. This would represent the idea of "nothing," and because it is not a number, it would, therefore, not be subject to the constraints of the rules of math, where zero fails its realness test and becomes impractical. This would also allow us to keep the negative and decimal number systems associated with everything from .99 down to negative one.

Next, we have the number 1, subjective/individual. This is the only number that is truly representational of the subjective/individual reality. Can you think of why?

Even/real number 2: This number is the representation of the natural/physical world in number theory. Evidenced by the name, "even number," everything is equal. It is all logical. It makes sense.

Think about our three-dimensional world. Even this concept is wrought with twos. We live in three dimensions, but you can go two directions in each dimension. You can move side to side (two), backward or forward (two), or up and down (two).

Odd/prime number 3: This represents the supernatural/extraphysical. Think odd and prime. What is odd about the number three? What is prime about it? Think about it. This definition differs to that of traditional prime numbers to include any number divisible by itself, 1, or any other odd/prime number (3, 5, 7, 9, 11, 13, 15, 17 are examples). Under these new definitions 9 and 15 become prime numbers as well. Or we can just keep calling them odd!

In conclusion, there are really only four numbers, and one of them is fake: 0. Numbers 1, 2, and 3 are the only real numbers, and all other numbers are a result of one or more math functions being used on two or more of the reality numbers.

5. Laws

a. Addition/Subtraction

Any real number added or subtracted to any real number gives you a real number (e.g., 2+2=4, 4+2=6, 6+2=8). This shows you can never attain the extraphysical through solely physical means.

Any real number added to any prime number gives you a prime number (e.g., 2+3=5, 5+2=7, 7+2=9). This shows with the inclusion of a prime number, you can achieve the prime through partially physical means.

Any prime number added to a prime number gives you a real number (e.g., 3+3=6, *6+3=9*, 9+3=12). This shows the physical reality of the function of addition/subtraction.

Any real number added to any imaginary number reflects itself, 2+0=2

Any real number subtracted by itself give you nil or nothing—not zero!

b. Multiplication

Any prime number multiplied by a prime number equals a prime number (e.g., 3×3=9, 9×3=27, 27×3=81). This shows the prime influence of the supernatural/extraphysical reality. It is self-sufficient. Needs nothing else.

Any prime number multiplied by a real number equals a real number (e.g., 3×2=6, 6×3=18, 18×3=54). This shows trying to multiply the extraphysical with the physical will only ever lead to the physical. The physical restrictions of the answer based upon the inclusion of a lesser physical number into the function.

Any real number multiplied by a real number equals a real number (e.g., 2×2=4, 4×2=8, 8×2=16). This shows you cannot get to the extraphysical reality by solely real means, there must be a prime number involved. Notice the difference between this last law of multiplication and the last law of addition/subtraction.

Any prime added to any prime gives you a real number; whereas you might expect a similar rule for multiplication, any real multiplied by any real gives you a prime, but notice that is not the case. Any real number multiplied by any other real number will always give you a real number; thus without the existence of the extraphysical, the concept of reality breaks down.

This would be a good time to talk about Yeshua and how he proved to be God of the physical world in the Bible. On numerous occasions, Yeshua not only showed a mastery of the physical world, but the ability to multiply, *through* division, the Bread and Fish Miracle.

Yeshua showed he was above the laws of math by feeding the five thousand with the few loaves and two fish. His walking on water was another way He showed His dominion over the physical. He divided in order to multiply to feed the hungry in the physical world. Spectacular!

c. Division

The three answers of division. Because the subjective reality deconstructs, when we divide, we will always get one of three types of answers based on the number reality and function being performed. A simple fractionalized number, (i.e., 1.5), a fractionalized repeater, (i.e., 1.3 repeating), or a whole number (2, 4, 6, 8, 10, etc.).

Any prime number divided by a prime number larger than itself equals a fractionalized repeater, indications of division function (i.e., fraction-introspection-subjectivity), and number (prime-infinity-repeating), even/real fraction (indicative of physical necessity of tri-real aspect), or a long, complicated, repeating fraction. For example, 3/5=0.6, 3/7=0.42857143, 3/9=0.3 (repeating), indicative of square roots. These answers seem to repeat going from an even fraction, to a more complicated repeating fraction, to a simpler repeating fraction.

Any prime number divided by a prime number smaller than itself will also equal either a whole number, an infinite repeating fraction, or an even fraction (e.g., 11/9=1.2 (repeating), 11/7= 1.57142857, 11/5=2.2, 11/3=3.6 (repeating), 11/1=11).

The Rosie Grace Wake-Up Song

I wrote this for my daughter when she was born. I sing it to her when she wakes up, most days. I just wanted to publish it.

When I arose
I pick a rose
For my little Presley Rose
Bring it in to her bed
Lay it by her sleepy head.
Warm embrace
Show your face
You're my little Rosie Grace
Let's pray
And give thanks
So that we can start the day!
(Insert on-the-spot-prayer like:
Dear Yeshua
Thank You for all Your love, Amen)
Now let's go and get some clothes
For my little Presley Rose
Even though it's not that cold
We still dress from head to toe!
Clothes are on
Now let's move on
My little Rosie Grace Clifton
Ahead, there's a big day
So we gotta end this song!

The Pitch

If you are planning on buying a copy or two of this book to give away as gifts, first off, I want to say thank you. I worked on this manuscript harder and more determinedly than I have worked on anything else in my entire life. I've always had a knack for writing, but until Yeshua found me, I never had anything to say that was important enough to motivate me to write a book.

I hope what I have written becomes a legitimate grassroots phenomenon and a million people read these words. But more than that, my sincere hope is that the concepts and ideas presented in this work have given you a better understanding and comprehension of the truth of God and Christ. If I have done that, I have accomplished my goal.

A million people probably won't read this book. Will a hundred people purchase two copies for others? Maybe. Maybe not. Even if only ten people care enough to buy only a single copy for someone else, those who do want to can find it at ChristainFaithPublishing. com. There you can search for the title of this book, *I. Witness*, and find links to where you can buy a copy or two.

No matter what, if you do decide to buy even a single copy for another person in your life, no matter how you do it, I want to thank you from the bottom of my heart for doing so. I did not write this book for the money, but whatever income I do generate from sales, I will feel like I have earned. So again, thank you for your support. God bless you! Now go read the Bible!

CPSIA information can be obtained
at www.ICGtesting.com
Printed in the USA
JSHW032122220522
26116JS00002B/7

9 781685 172657